Terry

Wagon

Enjoy the journey

Tom Benoit

A Struggle for Acceptance

Tom Benoit

Contents

Also by Tom Benoit

Reflections: The untold story of an uncommon man

Just Desserts: A memoir of Mary Benoit

In memory of my Mother, Mary Lorraine Benoit
and my Father, Armand Maurice Benoit

*

To my family, the source of my strength.

Prologue

JOHN SPENCER, M.D. spoke from the podium, "Welcome. My name is John Spencer, Chief of Pathology at Charlotte Memorial Hospital. The Administration let me out of the morgue to acquaint you with a special speaker today, a physician who has been given membership in the Mecklenburg Medical Society and our Medical Staff. You know whether battling a spreading infectious bug or fighting a hidden enemy in the steaming jungles of Central America, I found an essential quality is perseverance. Winston Churchill perhaps said it best in 1941, when speaking to the boys at the Harrow school where he once attended, 'Never give in, never, never, never, never - in nothing big or small, large, or petty - never give in except to convictions of honor and good sense!' Today it is my privilege to introduce Doctor Herman Jackson, who exemplifies the grit and determination of a physician who did not give up."

After a slight applause, the last seats in the Hospital's auditorium filled as Herman Jackson MD, a black physician, walked to the podium, slightly bent over, stepping forward like a man who had overcome a heavy burden. Yet, as he smiled and looked over at the audience of distinguished guests, he felt sure of himself. The auditorium was filled with doctors from all over, but mostly from Charlotte, North Carolina. The weight of all those eyes fell upon him. Herman Jackson, M.D. knew the audience could not believe this day was possible, that a black physician, the first to be accepted in the Mecklenburg Medical Society after all these years, had risen to speak.

The tranquility of the moment was broken periodically by a burst of noise that entered whenever the back door of the Hospital's auditorium opened. From the corridor came sounds of nurses walking, stretchers rolling by, and the intercom paging a doctor to the emergency room. This was the prestigious Charlotte Memorial Hospital. Proudly displayed, beneath a glimmering tower of glass and steel, was a spacious lobby decorated with furniture suitable for an upper-crust mansion. The hospital possessed the latest expensive medical equipment, and its halls were adorned with paintings of past presidents of the medical staff.

Herman gripped the podium with both hands. He nodded, the veins in his neck bulging slightly. Today he would need no notes. What he had to say would be guided by his convictions and a higher calling. For days, as he had considered this opportunity to speak, and now, as he looked over the audience, the leadership of the medical profession of Charlotte, many with gray hair, some with a stethoscope in their coat pocket, Herman Jackson M.D. thought of his past and how he got here.

He remembered growing up in Keystone, West Virginia in a 3-room shack with a metal roof that sounded like a machine gun's rapid-fire during hailstorms. The kitchen had a wood-burning stove, a large wooden table that Jacob, his father, made, and an icebox, mostly empty. Two bedrooms were off the kitchen, one for Jacob and Betsy, Herman's mother. The other was occupied by Herman, his brother Ruffas, and his two sisters, Grace, and Elizabeth, all of whom slept in bunk beds.

The home was filled with laughter and storytelling that Ruffas was especially good at. One evening, Herman recalled, Ruffas told a personal tale to Grace, Elizabeth, and him. It sent a chill down the backs of the Jackson kids. "After dark," Ruffas said, "I was out on my hands and knees in the grass gathering nightcrawler worms to go fishing the next day. There was an angry wind rattling leaves from nearby trees. The moon lit up the ground making spotting and capturing worms easier. Black clouds rolled by every now and then partially blocking the moon like a nighttime bear crossing the sky. A bolt of lightning sent its zagged arrow over the hilltop. Off in the distance mixed with the crack of thunder, I heard several horses galloping and men hollering. I stumbled to my feet and hid behind a tree. Bending my head slowly, I looked up and saw one of the men with dark long hair and a beard dismount. He took two boards and made a cross. After sticking it into the ground, he lit it on fire. I smelled its ugly oily flames curling with black smoke as the night riders, yelling words I had never heard before, rode around it several times before leaving." The Jackson kids were not sure what the burning cross meant, but they were sure it was not like the Easter sunrise service their parents took them to with a cross, and ladies all dressed up with their finest hats.

Ruffas was tall and lanky, fast as a runner. He was a good athlete who during another time might have received a college scholarship to be on the track team. But times were different for poor colored boys. There was limited time to practice or to play with white athletes. Ruffas liked to show local kids how to fish, run, or help them with their homework. He wanted to be a teacher like his father, but he never received any financial help, so furthering his education was out of the question. Ruffas took a job after high school in construction when the family moved to Charlotte, North Carolina.

Herman recalled his sisters were close. Their constant chattering at bedtime, from one bunk bed to another was like crows squawking. The talk would go on forever until Herman put the hammer down by yelling at them to shut up or he was going to cut their hair off.

Occupying the top bunk was Grace, whose round face was a light chocolate color, often accentuated by a wide smile framed by curly dark hair. Grace's tresses, like her mother's, had traces of auburn that gleamed like smoldering coals in a campfire. She played ball with her brothers, climbed trees, and did not shy away from putting worms on fishing hooks. Grace was the last to stop playing and to come in for dinner. At school, she was quick to question her teachers. "Why," seemed to be her favorite word, like, "Why no white boys come to our school?" Her tendency to challenge the status quo often resulted in Grace standing up for her classmates who were not popular. Her hand on a less emotionally secure student's shoulder, a gentle hug, a kind encouraging word, were actions that would foretell her eventual vocation as a nurse.

Elizabeth, occupying the lower bunk, was tall, which made her seem older than other children of her age. She had big brown eyes and liked to wear her hair short. Elizabeth often helped her mother around the house, appearing effortlessly like an eagle flying and humming a tune. She would not let on whether she was having problems at school, or elsewhere as local customs collided with her gentle worldview.

One day accompanying her mother to a department store in Uptown Charlotte, Elizabeth went to try on a dress, entering the closest changing room she saw. Abruptly Elizabeth was told by the salesclerk, "Don't you know, girl, that's a changing room for white folks. Over there is one for you colored folks!"

Elizabeth just said to the lady she was sorry, and to her mother whispered, "It don't pay me no never mind."

Her mother, Betsy, however, tossed the dress onto a display of blouses, and yanking Elizabeth's arm, led her out of the store. As a harbinger of an oncoming storm, it was a dark cloud - just one bigoted, hurtful action - with many more to visit the Jackson family as they grew up.

Herman, today, however, was not guided by the obstacles of the past. He stood steel erect, confident that the trials he and his ancestors had faced had given him the strength to endure any future hardship. Furthermore, overcoming such obstacles and prejudices, like a summit of a mountain subdued, would open the door to dreams yet unfulfilled. His smile of faith quietly filled the room with soothing comfort, like a mother tucking her child into bed for the night. Now he would accept the honor of membership in the Medical Society and relate the need of improving the community's health by expanding access to primary care. As an infectious disease specialist, he also planned to stress the importance of being prepared for the next epidemic before it became a major pandemic.

Chapter One

A MEDICAL MAVERICK

THE LETTERS ON the door in black proclaimed the office belonged to John J. Spencer M.D., Chief of Pathology, but my friends just called me Jake, a nickname given to me by my father early in life because he liked the manly sound of it. Dad was an orthopedic surgeon, working from sun-up to sun-down, focused on that part of the body he was going to make better. My dad had little time for anything else, no hobbies, and little socialization with friends or other doctors. As far as he was concerned, I could choose any career I liked as long as I became a surgeon, preferably one who dealt with bones. Perhaps to spite my Dad, I gave up carving the living to devote my energies to doing autopsies and examining tissues of the dead.

I did not however pursue my chosen career in medicine in a straight line. During my senior year in high school, after a night of drinking to douse my jealous rage upon seeing my girl with a friend, I got into a nasty car accident resulting in a severe injury to a young boy. I was arrested and spent a night in jail. The next day neither my father nor Judge Henderson showed any sympathy. I was given a choice: 90 days in jail or enlisting in the military. In a continuation of my depressed mood, I decided to let the U.S. Marines inflict some influential pain on me while they tried to straighten me out. What the hell, I deserved it.

I was soon taking a train to Parris Island, South Carolina to endure many weeks of what the Marines called "boot camp," but I called it pure hell. It was boiling hot in August, enduring mean ass sergeants screaming, showering my face with their spit, making me run in full battle gear for miles, then crawling through swamp mud. It broke me down. My adolescent cockiness fell off me like a snake shedding its skin.

Following my initial training, I was sent to Nicaragua, where a small force of Marines was trying to tilt a civil war between leftist insurgents and conservatives towards our interests. By holding the harbor and flying reconnaissance flights, the Marines were putting their thumb on the conflict's scale until a negotiated settlement could be reached.

After two years in the Marines, I no longer was in it just to feel the pain. The code of honor of the Marines impressed me. My desire to contribute to their mission led me to apply and be accepted to the Marine Officer Candidate School, OCS, in Quantico, Virginia. At the OCS, without realizing it, the Marine courses in moral and ethical leadership branded my character and commitment to serve others. "Ductus Exemplo," for The U.S. Marines, meant to lead more by example than reason, no matter what the personal sacrifice or what others may do. The grit developed as a Marine grunt became "Semper Fidelis," always faithful, in me as an officer. And it would be lived out further by eventually becoming a physician's physician, giving honest opinions that would help in the treatment of patients.

Upon leaving the Marines my interest in biology and anatomy started early, fascinated by the internal organs of a shark, a mouse, or a frog. Biology class gave way to inorganic and organic chemistry, and anatomy instruction at Vanderbilt University, in Nashville, Tennessee, Medical School at McGill University in

Montreal Canada, and Residency in Pathology at Saint Peters Hospital in Charlotte, North Carolina.

My pursuit of knowledge about the causes of death also helped the living; not by focusing just on one patient, but by considering similarities of patients who died, I came to understand diseases that afflict entire populations. I got more out of such observations than trying to work my way up the medical totem pole to become president of a hospital's medical staff. Kissing ass with a hospital administrator or medical leadership to get to be the top dog is not my cup of tea.

Enough about me. I wanted y'all to know that I have the background to recognize an accomplished person and physician. Being a native of Charlotte, a former leader of Marines, and an observant pathologist, I have appreciated how our city and our medical community have changed because of the unselfish determination of a young physician. He is also a Charlotte original. A man who, like a sailor faced with an unpredictable storm, charted a course right through it, teaching us all a valuable lesson that improved our collective health. His name is Herman Jackson, M.D..

Dr. Jackson was born in 1914 and he grew up dirt poor first in West Virginia and then in the Brooklyn area in the Third Ward in Charlotte, North Carolina. The Third Ward was the area in Charlotte where the Negroes lived, went to school, and worked. Not much has changed there. Negroes got their freedom. They weren't slaves anymore. Some were sharecroppers, who worked out to be the same. They worked the land, got food and a two-room shack to live in from the landowner, and a production quota by which they were to share in the profits if the farm exceeded its quota. Never happened though, as the landowner kept the books. The Negroes had the freedom to leave, but if they did, they had to pay to have their shack cleaned and repaired, which prevented them from moving. It was a hard life.

Other Negroes worked in the flour mills. Work was hard there; hot as hell in the summer shoveling grain into the bins to be ground into flour. Negroes could be seen wearing bandanas to shield them from the dust. Wages were barely enough to raise a family in the poorly constructed housing of the Third Ward.

The depression made matters even worse. Demand for finished goods was down, resulting in many being laid off. The bread lines at Saint Ann's Church stretched around the block. Men with nothing to do but bear the weight of not being able to feed their families stood with their heads bowed on street corners, like cattle waiting to be slaughtered. They shared bottles of whiskey and rumors of who might be hiring for a day's labor. Mostly they existed, too embarrassed to go home, the weight of shame filling their shoes. Any motivation they might have had was oozing off them like sap dripping off a tree.

It was out of this whirlpool of misery and hopeless dreams that this doctor, Herman Jackson, M.D. would rock the medical and social establishment of Charlotte, as well as the nation, to its core. I am the proud ex-Marine son of a bitch that helped light the fire, as you will soon learn from the life story of Herman Jackson, M.D.!

Chapter Two

THE BEGINNING:
A PLANTATION'S SAVIOR

THIS STORY BEGINS with Herman Jackson's grandfather, John, who was tall, broad-shouldered, slim at the waist, with clear brown eyes and a ready smile. He was born in 1843, in Mecklenburg County, North Carolina in a shack on the White Oak Plantation. William Johnson, a local hero who was a captain in the North Carolina militia, built the plantation which was John's first home. William had gained a fearless reputation at the Battle of King's Mountain, which was part of the American War of Independence. The Battle of King's Mountain was a military battle between the Patriots, who wanted America to be free, and the Loyalist militia, who wanted to remain part of Great Britain. At that conflict, Charlotte's Patriots shooting from behind trees rained bullets down on the redcoats and the Loyalists.

"Why stay with the Crown?" Patriots often shouted at their Loyalist neighbors. The Loyalists had their reasons. They had a long attachment to Britain because of family or business ties. They felt the need for order and believed the Crown was the legitimate authority, and that they would preserve the Loyalists' local customs, business interests, and way of life on southern plantations. Some Loyalists were weak and needed an outside defender such as the British. Other Loyalists of color were seduced by the British's promises of freedom from slavery, which made both some Patriots and some Loyalists nervous. If colored folks became free, how would it affect the economy and social standing of others in society?

The Battle of King's Mountain took place in 1780. The Patriots defeated the Loyalist's militia commanded by the British major, Patrick Ferguson. The unexpected victory of the Patriots militia over the Loyalists occurred after the British General, Lord Cornwallis, had defeated the Patriots many times. It was generally felt that Patriot's success at King's Mountain changed the course of the War. The British strategy of dividing the colonies to maintain their cotton and tobacco trade with the South was based on the erroneous assumption that the Loyalists would defeat the Patriots with little help. But the plantation Loyalists were no match for the Patriots, who were used to hunting and were growing in numbers. The Battle of King's Mountain greatly raised the spirits of the Patriots and became a rallying cry that drove Cornwallis out of North Carolina. Then Lord Cornwallis, with his army weakened, without sufficient reinforcements by the Loyalists, after a series of other skirmishes, retreated to Yorktown where he surrendered. It became the defining event of the Revolutionary War that led to the Treaty of Paris and independence for the thirteen colonies.

✧ ✧ ✧

The White Oak Plantation

Because John Jackson had a knack for repairing things like plows, wagon wheels, and guns, he was indispensable to George, the white overseer of the plantation. George, however, resented that the other Negroes looked up to John because of his independent spirit and steel strength of character. George told his foreman,

Jimmy, "I know one day I will have to break John, as I have with all the other free-spirited niggers to keep them in line."

George was used to having his way with the young colored ladies. Often, he would invite his pals from the nearby Beaver Dam Plantation over to his place to join him in dipping into the dark world of living out their fantasies. John was repulsed by the actions of George and his friends, satisfying their pleasures while increasing the number of slaves. Their White wives cast a blind eye to what was going on. Everyone White was content with the status quo. But not so the slaves, and especially not John, who often could be seen punching a wall after witnessing the degradation of the colored women. Something had to be done, and as sure as the rooster announced the coming of the dawn - he would act.

Knowing when George and his buddies were going to have their parties was an advantage for John. He could plan his resistance. One thing John could count on was that these White boys were highly superstitious. Like a bat avoiding the light of the day, they would stay away if something did not smell right. A foul odor could mean that there was an evil spirit around the Negro girls – best leave them alone. Loretta, a young colored girl who was particularly fond of John, was alone one night. To protect her and the other colored ladies, John devised a plan. John trapped two skunks and put them under the shacks of Loretta and the other young ladies, urging them to endure the smell and stay in the shacks. When George and his buddies came, they were repulsed by the odor and went running away screaming, "Ooeei," and "J'ees, George, this place is haunted!"

At another time, the night before George's monthly party, John gave Loretta some onions for the colored girls to put near their eyes so they would water, instructing them to scratch themselves as if they had some catchy illness. It worked. When George came into the ladies' shack and saw them all scratching with watery eyes, he bolted, telling his buddies, "Get the hell out of here! Niggers must have some kind of plague."

Then John, through Loretta, planted a seed with George's wife, Suzanna, that the Negro girls had some kind of contagious disease - best the menfolk stay away, lest they bring some ailment home.

19

Having a disposition that the overseer did not like resulted in John getting the taste of the whip. Forty lashes, which the White boys must have taken from the bible, were handed out regularly, like giving candy to their kids. The back of John showed the horror of the lashes, like an ink tattoo, and lay witness to his independent streak.

Loretta and John grew closer together. They were careful, however, not to be seen together, because it was common knowledge only the overseer or owner could arrange a mating - done by design often to breed certain traits like strength into any offspring. Whenever John and Loretta could make it away, they fell into each other's arms, like a rising tide with increasing intensity, sharing a common antithesis for the mistreatment of their brothers and sisters on the plantation, aware that nothing was going to change. Increasingly as they saw the beatings or felt the whip themselves, they knew that running was their only option.

Running was risky. Overseers of plantations often hired slave catchers, who were given great latitude in their pursuit of runaways by laws like the Fugitive Slave Act. This law mandated slaves be returned to their owners, even if they were in a free state. Bounty hunters could go anywhere, search any house without a warrant, detain and return anyone they considered a runaway to their owners or sell them. Often there was little to prove an individual grabbed was the runaway the bounty hunters we're pursuing. Many of the free Negroes were kidnapped and sold into slavery in the South that way. Once caught, slaves could be beaten to death, their screams as an example to stay put - like a dog in quicksand, slowly sinking, dying.

On a night with a full moon to guide their way, John and Loretta decided to run. But where would be safe? Mexico may have been an option since they had abolished slavery in 1820. Many slaves, though, did not know about Mexico; and if they did, traveling there through southern states would have been very dangerous. Some runaways from Georgia may have traveled to Saint Augustine, Florida, a Spanish territory where they may have been welcomed. But to get to Florida would require traveling through too much hostile territory. Canada, they decided, was their goal. It abolished slavery in 1834.

John and Loretta departed late that night, slogging through swamps to hide their passage, tripping over unforeseen roots, brushing off leeches and mosquitoes, hearing the owls, constantly watching for snakes – always guided by the North Star - to go where they could show their feelings for each other without the scourge of the whip.

"Have faith, trust in me. I have contacts with abolitionists in the Underground Railroad. They will help us. But now, we must put distance between the bounty hunter's dogs and ourselves." John said.

Faster and faster, they ran. John and Loretta first stopped near Cowans Ford on the Catawba River near present-day Lake Norman, North Carolina. There they encountered Peter Griswold, who offered a bed and a hot meal of biscuits and beef stew. For passage to Raleigh, North Carolina, they hid in the back of a carriage. Like a frightened possum, they lay still to avoid discovery. Then they met up with another abolitionist, Benjamin Grover, who as a Presbyterian minister abhorred the very idea of slavery. "Knowing how the Lord accepted all people, tax collectors, and prostitutes alike, how can you claim to be a good Christian, while enslaving others just because their tan is darker than ours?" Benjamin urged other ministers in the South to take up the cause and support the antislavery movement, but he was generally unsuccessful. He wondered, as did the former slave and statesman, Frederick Douglas, why the Christian ministry in America did not strongly support the abolitionists as church leaders in England had done many years before. In a speech relating to this matter, Frederick Douglass chided the clergy in the United States, who professed to be in favor of religious freedom while ignoring the fact that 3,000,000 slaves did not have the freedom to worship, marry who they wanted, receive an education, or move about. He was aware that Great Britain had financial ties to the slave trade. Yet they had passed laws abolishing the slave trade in 1807 because of the aggressive opposition to slavery by their religious leaders.

Next, John and Loretta jumped on a train that took them to Washington DC, where they were always looking over their shoulders for danger, knowing slave catchers could grab a runaway and return them for a handsome reward. Washington D.C. was in a state of flux, as the District's southern area of Alexandria was in economic decline, partly due to a lack of funding from Congress. Alexandria was a major market in the American slave trade. Fear that the abolitionists in Congress would end slavery had depressed the economy. The Virginia General Assembly voted to return all the Virginia land that had previously been donated to form the District of Columbia in a process known as retrocession. The remaining land in the District was only what had been donated by the State of Maryland.

To save money that they would need for travel, John and Loretta sought work. Free Blacks and slaves in the capital worked as housemaids, butlers, carriage drivers, and construction workers. John took a job as a day laborer while Loretta worked as a maid cooking meals for a wealthy family.

Colored folks in the District acted like chameleons' lizards, changing their image to blend with their surroundings. They could be seen looking down, walking as if reading something on the sidewalk. They were constantly alert and anxious, expecting the worst. Domestic slaves feared being sold to work in southern plantations, while runaways feared the slave catchers. Freedmen and freedwomen feared being kidnapped and then transported south into slavery. They were required to always have a copy on them of their Certificate of Freedom. Without their proof of freedom, Negroes could be jailed until they produced documentation and then would have to still pay the cost of their jail time or be sold into slavery.

After saving enough funds, John and Loretta decided to take a train from D.C. to Baltimore, then to Philadelphia, and finally to New York City. Such a journey required them to obtain papers showing that they were free. John had an idea. If he could only find a freed colored man working for the Washington Union newspaper, it might be possible to print papers that would pass as Certificates of Freedom. After a few days of research, John met

Jason Carlson, who was able to forge papers good enough to pass muster, once they were roughed up by John to look older. John showed them to Loretta, who smiled, realizing that the papers were just one step as they traveled what fugitive runaways called the great Underground Railroad, an organized arrangement of safe houses, trails, and assistance to help fugitive slaves.

John and Loretta boarded the Baltimore Philadelphia Train at 8 a.m. Loretta drew closer to John. Their trip proved to be full of ups and downs. Thirty-five miles north of Baltimore, passengers had to disembark from the train to cross the Susquehanna River by ferry. At Wilmington, they boarded a steamboat for Philadelphia. When they got off the ship, they had no idea how they were going to get to New York City. A colored man or woman asking too many questions might look suspicious. As they walked near the docks with their belongings, Loretta was about to show her independence. She wandered up to a colored man who was shouting while selling the Philadelphia Inquirer, "Read all about it, read all about it! John Brown's Raid on Harpers Ferry." Loretta bought the newspaper, and then, turning her head slightly, asked the man quietly, "How do we get to New York City?"

Suspecting that they may be fugitive slaves, the man looked around and said in a low voice, "Go down to Market Street, take the ferry across the Delaware River to Camden, New Jersey. Ride the Amboy Railroad to South Amboy, New Jersey. Then you must take another ferry across the Hudson River to a dock in New York City."

Loretta smiled and thanked the man for his help.

"You take care, honey. Makem sure you both stay away from the bagmen. They kidnap free and runaways alike, so they can suck money by selling colored folks to the pimps in the South," the man said with a wave of his hand and a wink in his eye.

After getting on the ferry, Loretta opened the Philadelphia Inquirer she had just bought. She read about the raid by John Brown, an abolitionist of Calvinist Faith, his three sons, and a band of twenty men that had overrun the United States arsenal at Harpers Ferry. Brown intended that the raid would lead to an armed insurrection of slaves and abolitionists, that would culminate in ending slavery in the United States. Brown's victory was short-lived. By morning, a company of United States Marines led by Colonel Robert E. Lee, a rising military leader who graduated second in his class at West Point Academy, had killed ten of Brown's men, including two of his sons. Brown was wounded, held for treason and murder by the State of Virginia. John, reading the article over Loretta's shoulders, held her tight. Like a rooster announcing the dawn, John knew that this event, Brown's raid on Harpers Ferry, was just a precursor of a bloody struggle that would rip the country apart. A compromise was now not an option. Two sides entrenched in righteous indignation were destined to spill their blood. When the storm clouds of war rose in the sky, each side had their seductive encouragement: liberty, freedom. Slavery would now be the cause of deadly battles between the northern and southern states, where sometimes brothers would be forced to fight each other.

Arriving in New York City, John and Lorretta wandered away from the dock down Market Street with their knapsacks over their shoulders, amazed at the sound of different languages they heard. Walking more upright now, they were less suspicious of bounty hunters, because they heard that New York City had outlawed slavery.

But it was also true that if you were already a slave in New York City, you stayed one. New York City had a love-hate affair with slavery. On the one hand, many of the leaders of the abolitionists lived in the city, and it was considered a key stop in the Underground Railroad for runaways traveling to Syracuse, New York, New Bedford, Massachusetts, or Canada. On the other hand, New York City had prospered because of the slave trade. They had made the financial arrangements for colored people to be purchased in West Africa and brought to the South and the Caribbean Islands for a fee.

In New York City there were networks of people who turned a blind eye to the kidnappers of freed Negros as well as the slave catchers, who grabbed colored folks and dragged them to the South. Colored sailors would go missing from docks. Children of color would disappear on their way home from school. Black servants who traveled into New York City with their employers found themselves kidnapped and sold against their will - disappearing into the deep South. People held in New York City's municipal prison cells would find themselves sold to slave traders by unscrupulous police officers. Police in New York City were notorious for running "kidnapping clubs." Other groups, led by the Abolitionists Society and the New York Committee of Vigilance, assisted escaped slaves, and prevented their re-enslavement.

Into this melting pot of people, with different views, incentives, and languages, John and Loretta navigated to a prominent activist, David Ruggles. David had boarded ships in the New York harbor to find and later free captured colored persons earmarked to be sold illegally into slavery. David was quick to assess John's character and then said, "Don't worry, I have connections. I can get you out of town."

"How and where?" John asked with his arm around Loretta.

Putting his hand on John's soldiers, David responded, "By train and then to a safe house in New Bedford, Massachusetts, considered to be the whaling capital of the world. You will be buttoned up out of danger until you can get a job in their expanding fishing industry. Then you can earn enough for your passage to Canada if you so desire.

John and Loretta thanked David, knowing that the journey ahead was still full of uncertainty and danger.

Chapter Three

ON FREEDOM'S ROAD

AFTER ARRIVING IN New Bedford, John and Loretta found the safe house to which David had directed them. The home was owned by Sean O'Connor. Sean was of medium height, slightly overweight, with red curly hair, a full beard, a round face, and an impish grin. His wife Laoise, like Sean, was an immigrant from Ireland. Laoise brushed her long strawberry blond hair from her blue eyes and walked to greet them with a slight limp because she was born with one leg shorter than the other. After introductions and stories about their journey, Laoise gave John and Loretta what she called, "shepherd's pie" and a pint of homemade ale.

Laoise said, "You two must be exhausted. Let me show you where you will be staying, which is safe and out of the way." She led them to the attic.

After putting away their meager belongings, John said to Loretta, "I am going to go down to the docks to see if I can find work. David told me that they may need a carpenter or a dockhand."

"OK, just do not end up being bagged and put on a ship going South," Loretta said, always worried that they would be separated.

As John came down the stairs, he saw Sean in the kitchen, who suggested to John, "Talk to a fellow down at the harbor named Liam Shaughnessy. He is a foreman there. Tell him I've sent ya. We Irish knows what it is like to face the headwinds of bigotry, and we have learned to stick together."

John met Liam, a short man in his forties, with broad shoulders, a potbelly, and arms that were thick and muscular, like limbs from a tree. Liam said, "I'ya, so Sean sent ya. He's good. Could use a man with a keen eye who can make barrels, wooden chests, and some decking on ships."

John eagerly said, "Then I am your man."

Liam took John under his wing, introducing him to his men, many of whom shared a common bond, having emigrated from Ireland during the potato famine of 1845 to 1852 and had suffered bad treatment by the British. They spoke in broken English mixed with Gaelic, often regaling stories about their past or fables that ended with laughter like a big wave crashing. John liked the camaraderie, and the pay allowed him to buy food and save for their future.

But John and Loretta were not content to live in New Bedford, Massachusetts for a long time. They still feared the danger of being kidnapped and sent back to the White Oak Plantation, to be beaten and killed as an example to other slaves to know their place. There was still the Fugitive Slave Act of 1850, by which owners could pursue their slaves and return them to bondage, even if the slaves were now in a free state. Numerous court cases and laws supported the property rights of slaveholders. John had been told even the Constitution of the United States in article IV had proclaimed:

"No person held to service or labor in one state, under the laws thereof, escaping into another, shall in consequence of any law or regulation, be discharged from such service or labor, but he'll be delivered upon a claim of the party to whom such services may be due."

He was told this article was instrumental in getting the Southern States to join the Union after the Revolutionary War and independence from Britain. Politicians speaking before Congress and lawyers prosecuting those abetting fugitives often cited this section of the Constitution. Even Abraham Lincoln, during his first inaugural address, John learned, mentioned that he would follow the Constitution regarding runaway slaves seeking freedom in non-slavery states, although he supported jury trials to determine the facts regarding a person's legal status.

✧　✧　✧

Six Months Later, New Bedford, Massachusetts

After working on the docks for half a year, John and Loretta secured passage on a ship bound for Nova Scotia, a part of Canada. Nova Scotia had originally been settled by the French in 1605. The British army, aided by the militia from Massachusetts, deported all the French-speaking people from 1755 to 1764 as part of the French and Indian War. In Nova Scotia, John and Loretta could, at last, breathe in the fresh air of freedom. Canada had been a beacon for fugitive slaves for some time. The Foreign Slave Trade Act passed by Brittan in 1807 prevented the importation of slaves by British traders into territories belonging to foreign powers. Then the British banned slavery throughout their colonies altogether in 1834.

John and Loretta settled in a town called Dartmouth and enjoyed going to the African Baptist Church in Halifax, established in 1832 by fugitive slaves. The churches in Nova Scotia gave shelter, food, and counseling to newly arrived slaves, many with little money, often in poor health, and with their wits frayed. John worked in the shipyard as a carpenter. Loretta rolled up her sleeves, pitching in to help teach school-age colored children, many of whom had never had any instruction. Illiteracy was the rule, and confidence was low among children, who previously were punished on southern plantations for just picking up a book.

Aiming to give some assurance, Loretta told one little eight-year-old girl, "Rosie, no one is better than you. You can learn to read and write because I am going to show you."

John and Loretta added to their income and food by fishing off the shore and picking blueberries, which were plentiful on the island. Life was good. There was a growing community of colored folks in Dartmouth and Halifax. They had made friends through the gatherings at the African Baptist Church. The house they lived in was small but adequate.

After a dinner of lobsters John obtained from a lobsterman as a trade for repairing a few traps, John grabbed Loretta's hand, pushed back the kitchen table, awkwardly put one knee on the floor, and proposed. "I want you to be my lifelong companion, my wife. Together we will raise children, who will live out their dreams."

For Loretta, it was seeing her hopes come true. Through all their struggles, she knew John was the man with whom she wanted to spend the rest of her life. She witnessed how John protected the colored women on the White Oak Plantation, made friends, and arranged for safe passage along the Underground Railroad. Loretta knew John would also be a good father. A few months later, on December 15, 1860, huddled together to keep warm as snow covered the landscape, John and Loretta were married at the African Baptist Church in Halifax with Reverend Richard Preston presiding.

Loretta and John continued to live in Dartmouth, Nova Scotia, John working in the shipyards, and Loretta helping in the school where children of African descent learned to become independent and thrive. They were mostly content but were troubled by the news back home. One Sunday, they read in the Liverpool Transport newspaper:

> *The only reason the South joined the Union was the U.S. Constitution guaranteeing the Southern States that any runaway slave property would be caught and returned! The Northern States, by aiding runaways, made, in the minds of slaveholders, a mockery out of those assurances. South Carolina decided to secede from the*

Union as soon as Abraham Lincoln was elected President. Six other southern States joined South Carolina. On April 12, 1861, Confederate troops bombarded Union soldiers at Fort Sumter, South Carolina. Soon four other Southern States joined the Confederacy.

Upon reading this, John proclaimed, "Now a bloody struggle will occur, and many slaves, once freed, will go to the Northern States."

✧   ✧   ✧

The United States, 1865

After over 600,000 deaths and the destruction of many of the southern cities like Richmond and Atlanta, the South surrendered on April 9, 1865. Diminished, Robert E. Lee, who, before becoming the leader of the Confederate forces, was once asked to be the commander of all the Union forces, surrendered his Army of Northern Virginia to Ulysses S. Grant at the McLean home, at Appomattox Court House, Virginia. The Civil War had left a scar on the body politic of the nation. The fighting had stopped, but the hostilities of the southern Whites towards their former chattel property, people of African descent, raged on.

Many former slaves migrated to the north, crowding together into the poorer sections of big cities. They found work any way they could to feed their families. Black women took jobs as maids or nannies taking care of the White children of those Whites who could afford it. The men had more difficulty finding something to do. As one freedman, Houston Holloway wrote, "Colored people did not know how to be free, and White people did not know how to have a free colored man around them."

Despite the Emancipation Proclamation in 1863, and two more years of the Civil War, in which former slaves fought, the country was unprepared for the aftermath. After the war there was the ratification of the Thirteenth Amendment in 1865 outlawing slavery; the passage of the Civil Rights Act of 1875 (later over-turned by the Supreme Court); the ratification of the Fourteenth Amendment in 1868 proclaiming no state could deny its citizens' due process or equal protection of the law; and the Fifteen Amendment ratified in 1870, granting that no state could deny the right to vote on account of race or color. Nevertheless, acceptance of former slaves as full citizens of the United States by the former Confederate States of America was difficult. Inconsistent progress was made both in the South and in the North. For one thing, to enforce emancipation and the civil rights of Blacks, it took Union troops entering former Confederate states at different time periods. Texas was the last state to declare an end to slavery on June 19, 1865, when Union General Gordon Granger informed Texans in Galveston that the Civil War had ended, and all slaves freed. Moreover, with each step forward the black freemen achieved, resentment grew among southern Whites, who were determined not to lose what they considered their position in society. The stage was set to curtail the rise of newly freed slaves by violence, separation, prejudices, and denial of rights.

The resourcefulness and persistence of former slaves at the time of the Reconstruction were aided by members of the Negro churches, missionaries, and teachers from the Northern States, who helped the freedmen with their literacy. Many former slaves took advantage of this opportunity to learn.

John and Loretta decided after a while to return to the United States and perhaps North Carolina. Although there were challenges back home in the South, the reason that they fled to Canada, their freedom, was no longer a magnet to keep them there. The climate in Nova Scotia was too harsh, and they longed to see the magnolias blossom. After the Civil War, life in Halifax, Nova Scotia became difficult. Crops regularly failed, and work at the docks decreased along with trade with the United States and Europe. The Elgin-Marcy treaty of 1854, between the United States and Britain, had expanded trade between Canada and the States, but after the Civil War, the protectionist sediments in the US and anger in America over the British supporting the Confederacy, led to the termination of the Treaty, resulting in less trade. Consequently, there was a decline in manufacturing employment in Canada, and shops there had fewer American-made goods. A decrease in goods transported between the two countries led to a reduction in shipping and work for John at the shipyard. As Canadians left Nova Scotia, it further depressed the economy.

Once their decision was made, the Jacksons wasted no time in boarding a ship that would take them to Virginia, then on to the Port of Wilmington, North Carolina, and finally by train to Charlotte. They rented a three-bedroom house, and John got a job as a carpenter repairing houses that had been neglected during the Civil War. Although many colored folks were migrating north to work in the factories located in the big cities, there were still many like John and Loretta, who stayed behind or were returning to the South, to start a new life. Charlotte's population was growing - nearly doubling in the 1860s. The City was leading the way in a New South. One that was less reliant upon agriculture, predominantly "king cotton" with its rural plantations, and more dependent upon urban industrialization, mirroring what was already occurring in the North.

Life for Negro families was a dichotomy. On the one hand, they were free; on the other hand, they were subjected to Jim Crow laws that began right after the Civil War ended, and was aggravated by the U.S. Supreme Court's ruling that the Civil Rights Act of 1875, forbidding discrimination in hotels, trains, and other public places was unconstitutional and not authorized by the 13 or 14th amendment of the Constitution. These laws were meant to marginalize colored people by denying them the right to vote or get a comparable education. There were also black codes and local laws that directed where Negros could work as well as what their compensation would be. These codes worked against the formerly enslaved people, often causing them to be incarcerated and hired out of prisons by local businesses to work in their farms and factories. When John saw groups of black prisoners working on repairing roads, he commented to Loretta, "Nothing has changed. They are treating us like slaves all over again."

For Negros living in North Carolina after the War, the danger was a part of everyday life. Negro schools and churches were vandalized, and bands of violent, angry Whites attacked, tortured, and lynched colored citizens in the night. The Ku Klux Klan, started in Tennessee by former Confederate soldiers, was one of the most notorious ruthless secret organizations targeting Negro communities. Jim Crow laws forbid descendants from Africa from entering parks, theaters, restaurants, waiting rooms for the bus terminals, using water fountains, restrooms, public schools, and hospitals. Marriage and public habitation between colored and Whites were strictly forbidden in every southern state.

Because of the hardship of living with Jim Crow laws and even though colored folks were treated far better in Charlotte than in the rest of the South, John and Loretta decided to move to Bluefield, West Virginia, wherein 1872, John heard that Concord College, near Princeton, West Virginia, was hiring mechanics for their Maintenance Department. John learned that the West Virginia legislature passed legislation that Concord College, founded by veterans of the Confederacy and the Union, needed workers because they were expanding and building dorms. John was familiar with West Virginia.

"There is an independent spirit there," he told Loretta, trying to sell his idea of going to Concord College. "I like the fact they broke away from Virginia a few years before the Civil War started, did not join the Confederacy, and there was not that much destruction in the state because of the War."

Once John and Loretta arrived in Bluefield, they went straight to the African Baptist Church on Main Street. John mentioned to Loretta, "Negro Churches are our saviors in times of need." Their Reverend Isaiah Thompson greeted and helped them find a place to stay. Not long after that, John found work at Concord College, located on a plateau in a beautiful mountain area in Concord Church, West Virginia. The College grew out of the "normal school" movement in the aftermath of the Civil War, developing teachers who would educate a mostly illiterate population. The legislature of West Virginia asked the town of Concord to build a courthouse, jail, and a school of higher learning at no cost to the State. The West Virginia "mountaineer spirit" of generosity was soon tapped, like sap flowing from a maple tree. William Martin donated the land, and $1,700 was raised - enough to erect a small wooden building. A former Captain in the Confederate Army, James Harvey French, served as the school's first principal. Later the legislature, impressed with the school's accomplishments, appropriated $5,000 to build another facility. The school's name evolved from the Normal School in Concord, West Virginia to Concord College. John's responsibilities grew with the school. He went from overseeing construction and general mechanic duties to the Superintendent of Facilities. John and Loretta were content to be helping many of the Negro students to learn and improve their lives. Loretta was doing domestic work with several of the area's wealthy families. The population of Bluefield was growing because of the expanding coal and timber industries. The Jacksons decided that the time was good to start a family. Jacob (who was to become Herman Jackson's father) was born in 1879.

Chapter Four

FATHER LIKE SON

IKE HIS FATHER, Jacob at an early age showed a strong desire to learn. When Dad went fishing and hunting, Jacob was quick to tag along, raising all sorts of questions. Like a drunk sitting on a bar stool, his thirst for learning was never quenched. This intellectual curiosity carried over during Jacob's education, as difficult as it was in West Virginia. For a colored boy, schooling was far from optimal. Looking back post-Civil War black education in the South can be divided into three phases. In the first part, some Whites were inclined to help Negroes with their education after the Civil War if the Negroes had served them well as slaves. Thus, in the beginning, the initial instructors of colored students were benevolent White teachers covering the basics of reading, writing, and some arithmetic. The second development of education came from missionary teachers sent out by the Freedmen Belief Commission and the Freedmen Bureau. These instructors rented shanty-like schoolhouses, and not only concretely raised the knowledge level of their pupils, but they also inspired the students to learn on their own and teach others of their race. Colored folks, as a result, motivated each other to learn.

The population of Negroes in West Virginia was growing towards the end of the nineteenth century. They found jobs in the coal industry that was expanding because West Virginia's coal was of high quality for making steel out of iron. More Negroes produced a shortage of teachers which resulted in the third phase of education in the Mountaineer State of West Virginia. To meet the need, teachers were recruited from the neighboring states of Maryland, Ohio, and Virginia. Such states had more colored teachers due to their liberal policies toward educating Negroes. Recently educated teachers from these states, moreover, were looking for work, since the climate of prejudices in their communities was not sufficiently low enough for them to teach White students. Hence, they flocked to West Virginia and its growing Negro population.

The influx of teachers fulfilled two important needs: they instructed colored pupils and they ministered to the general population, fostering their faith and hope. The incoming educators were instrumental in establishing most of the Baptist and Methodist churches in West Virginia. They could be seen teaching students during the week and preaching the gospel to them on Sundays.

State government support for free education in West Virginia for Negroes did not occur until the legislature passed a law providing for the establishment of schools for Negro students in 1866. Such schools to obtain funds had to have at least 16 students. If the number was below that limit, the schools were supposed to be closed. In 1872 the constitution of West Virginia was amended to mandate that schools for White and colored students must be separate. In Bluefield, West Virginia the first school for White students opened in 1889 and for colored pupils in 1890. In the third year, the school for colored pupils burned down. The school location was then moved to Cooperstown, West Virginia. After that school also burned down, the classroom facility was moved to Northern Bluefield, where many Negroes had settled. The school was in a barroom, then a pool room. Still, later the school was in a courthouse, before landing in a storeroom for three years.

Jacob was fortunate that his parents, John, and Loretta, had learned to read, even while in bondage. They became much better readers and proficient in writing and could do simple mathematics from classes in the Baptist Church in Nova Scotia, Canada. They used that knowledge to teach Jacob, who was eager to learn, no matter what the subject. When John and Loretta had exhausted what they could teach, they solicited the help of Reverend Bernard Goodman, who taught children in the back of his Baptist church in Bluefield. It was a collaborative effort, as Jacob learned as much from the older students as he did from Reverend Bernard. There was no dividing line or separation of the students according to grades. They helped each other with assignments and shared books, paper, and rudimentary writing instruments. The students sat on hard benches which were often cold. Dim sunlight entered the church's few windows on one side in the morning and on its other side in the afternoon. When it was cloudy outside and there was little light to read, Reverend Bernard did more talking. The students were respectful and well-behaved. Any deviation was met with an admonishment from the Reverend that they were in the house of God.

After six years Jacob went to the first public school for colored students, which was now located in an abandoned store in the northern area of Bluefield. He sat in the front of the class, always quick to raise his hand with an answer. Jacob also would frequently pose a question such as: what if this happens instead of that occurring. At times his inquiries stumped his teachers, converting the educators into pupils taking a hard oral exam. One night after Jacob was in his junior year of high school, the school caught fire and burned to ashes. No one knew the cause, but it was well known that there were elements of the population who did not want Negroes getting any meaningful education.

The public school for Negro children moved on an emergency basis to Cooperstown in Boone County, West Virginia. Getting to Cooperstown meant traveling along treacherous winding mountain roads through Beckley, West Virginia. A trip by carriage could take four hours. As a result, Jacob mostly taught himself for the remainder of his time in high school. He only went to the school in Cooperstown a few days a month to receive his textbooks and assignments.

During the time Jacob was studying at home, he liked to ride his bike to Concord College. He rode carefully because the roads were poor with big ditches on either side, inviting a trip down the mountain for anyone who ventured off the road. Jacob liked to walk around the campus, pass the brick education building, the cafeteria, and end up at the library. There he would emerge himself reading books and newspapers. He would look for books that would help him with his studies. Sometimes he would even sit in the back of a classroom and listen to a lecture. *Why not,* Jacob thought, *my father, is the Superintendent of Facilities.*

After graduating from high school, Jacob applied to Concord College. Due to his good grades and his father's position, Jacob received a partial scholarship. Jacob chose Concord College because of its reputation for raising the literacy levels and capabilities of students. Jacob wanted to be a teacher so he could help poor colored children, who, like him, struggled in segregated schools with worn-out books.

On the opening day of freshman year in 1897, John and Loretta hitched up their carriage and drove Jacob to Concord College for his orientation and the first day of classes. John said to Loretta, "Each freshman class has more and more students of color." They felt Jacob would have a sense of camaraderie that would soften the blows of prejudice that they were sure he would encounter.

Sometimes Jacob experienced subtle forms of racism, like when White students would not sit next to him in class. At other times it was starker, for example when he went to lunch and sat down at a table occupied by three White guys from his English class. Across from him sat Johnny, who had light brown hair and a stocky build. He appeared to be leading most of the conversation. His father worked at Bluefield Hospital. Sitting in the middle was Robert, short and overweight with blond curly hair. His parents owned a coal mine in McDowell County. Like many of the coal barons, they lived in Bluefield because the cultural activities there were far superior to living in the rural areas where coal was mined. Jacob knew from hearing him in class that Robert liked to talk about mining, his parents' big car, and what he did on his vacations at their summer home in Myrtle Beach, North Carolina. Carl, eating the staple West Virginia lunch of cornbread and pinto beans, had a girlfriend named Bobby Jo, who occupied his thoughts and life when he was not in school.

Jacob said to them, "That sure was a lot of homework Mrs. Radford gave us," and the students, without saying a word, rose and moved to another table. Jacob tried to not let it bother him. From the kitchen, he smelled fried chicken. He heard the laughter of White students, making him feel lonely as if he was marooned on some deserted island. Looking around deep in thought, he noticed slivers of yellow light coming through the windows as the sun shone through a break in the cloudy noonday sky. The shadows lifted from over the nearby mountains. He thought, *why are some people so afraid to treat others as they would like to be treated? Are they scared about what others in their group will say? Are they so insecure in their shoes that they fear reaching out to a Negro? Will that lessen their standing? These mistreatments,* Jacob realized, *are strengthening my desire to build confidence in young people of all races. White and Black students can chart a new course by abandoning the prejudices of their ancestors and peers, finding happiness in learning, and becoming independent thinkers. Raising confidence will be my life's quest! Becoming a teacher of young adults will be how I fulfill it!*

Jacob, having finished his lunch, still the only one at his table, smiled, drew in a big breath of air, filled his chest like a bullfrog, and stood up with his posture erect. He walked away from the table past the three White students, like a ten-point buck walking through the forest. Jacob had used this event to find himself.

✧　✧　✧

Graduation Day

After four arduous years, Jacob was ready to graduate from Concord College. The day was slightly overcast, with the sun trying to climb over the nearby knoll. In the courtyard, there was a stage constructed so graduates could walk up and receive their diplomas. White chairs were arranged in parallel straight rows for students and their parents. John and Lorretta sat on each side of Jacob, alternatively patting their arms on his shoulders, and smiling. A close observer might have seen water forming in the corners of their eyes. Everyone recited the pledge of allegiance, then sat down and the school band played "Pomp and Circumstance," a tune composed in 1901 by Edward Edgar for the coronation of Edward VII. (It was played again when Edward walked across the stage as he received an honorary doctorate degree at Yale University.)

The President of the College, Arthur Thorn, spoke, "Today we leave behind differences, struggles of the past, and form a new bond, with opportunity and progress as our goal. You have mastered your subjects and are now ready to enter the world of promise." President Thorn went on optimistically about the students' future and the State of West Virginia's prospects. He added, "We escaped much of the destruction and post-war acrimony of the Civil War. The Mountain State is blessed with abundant natural resources, as well as our mountaineer spirit. The degree to which we move forward as a state will be dependent upon graduates like you."

✧　✧　✧

Teaching High School Students

Jacob went on after graduation from Concord College to teach American History at Bluefield High School. Walking to his class at Bluefield High, Jacob noticed storm clouds the color of soot. He put his collar up and tucked his books under his arms. Quickening his steps, he got into the school before the rain came. Despite the gloomy weather, Jacob appreciated the moment. He liked history and knew that teaching students about West Virginia's can-do spirit, and how the United States struggled and evolved, could give his pupils confidence in their abilities.

As the only Negro teacher at the school, Jacob was careful to present information in a nonpolitical way. He began teaching US History by telling his students about their home state. "West Virginia, by breaking away from Virginia during the Civil War, was the only state to be formed from a Confederate state. Our state's "Mountaineer spirit" grew out of a feeling to do things independently," Jacob continued. "West Virginia was part of the British colony founded in 1607, until it became part of the State of Virginia in 1776, one of the original thirteen colonies. Residents of the colonies were divided between the Patriots, who wanted to break away from Britain, and the Loyalists, who wanted to stay under British rule. The Patriots were opposed to the taxes levied against them by the British. England taxed the colonists to assist with all the debts that Britain had incurred because of the French and Indian War."

"How did the French and Indian war start?" one of his students, James, asked attentively.

"It was a conflict between the French and British that began with many years of wars between the two in Europe and then spread to the New World. In North America, there was rivalry over who would control the trade in the Ohio River Valley. Both the French with their Indian allies and the British with their settlers from the thirteen colonies claimed ownership of the area. After a long struggle, Britain won the conflict, amassing large debts. In the Treaty of Paris in 1863 France ceded Canada and their whole North American Empire to Britain."

A student, skinny as a toothpick with long curly brown hair, shouted a question, "After the war were the colonists and the British one happy family?"

"No," Jacob said, pausing with his hand on his chin for a moment to give weight to what he wanted to say. "The militias from the thirteen colonies by fighting gained a sense of unity among themselves and anger against the British."

"Why was that?" asked a young girl student abruptly without raising her hand.

"The colonial militia resented the fact they were doing all the fighting and dying for what was essentially a conflict between the French and the British. The French and Indian War resulted in mistrust between the colonists and the British rulers," Jacob said, "that was hidden below the surface, kind of like a snake moving slowly beneath wet leaves. Adding fuel to the fire, the English parliament thought the colonists did not pay enough to support the war effort. So, Britain, being heavy in debt because of their wars in Europe and America, decided, without consulting the colonial legislature, to impose taxes. Hence resentment gave birth to the slogan 'no taxation without representation.' The colonists boycotted British goods. When the British imposed a tax on tea, the 'Sons of Liberty dumped tons of tea from a ship into Boston Harbor."

"So, what happened next?" A student, James, asked. His classmates, now leaning forward, all eyes upfront, were silent, like deer watching for a sound.

Jacob looked at his watch and then related how the Revolutionary War began. "Thomas Gage, the governor the British had installed in Massachusetts, fearing a conflict with the colonists, asked the Crown for more troops to be stationed there. The British did not want to foot the bill for more military personnel. The British instructed the Governor to seize the colonists' arsenal. The colonists, however, blocked the British troops as they advanced towards Concord, Massachusetts, and fought the first military battle of the American War of Independence. Afterward, the Continental Army was formed under the leadership of George Washington, who the British knew because of his courageous leadership during the French and Indian War." Jacob asked the class to read the next two chapters in their book covering both the Revolutionary War and the Civil War as homework.

✧　✧　✧

One day towards the end of the school year Jacob was in the backyard under the leaves of a large oak tree reading his students' essay papers. His mother came waving the Bluefield Daily Telegraph. "Jacob," she exclaimed, "guess what? The Bluefield Colored Institute is looking for an Assistant Professor to teach American History and English. Maybe you should apply."

Jacob put down the papers he was correcting. *Why not,* he thought, *I know as much about the subject as anybody, and the Institute is located nearby.* "Okay, it can't hurt. Give me the address, and I will apply."

Bluefield Colored Institute started in 1815 as a college to train Negro students to be teachers. Its first Principal was Hamilton Hatter, who oversaw the construction of several buildings. (In 1906 Robert Sims took over and led the College for three decades. In 1932 Bluefield Colored Institute changed its name to Bluefield State Teachers College, and in 1943 to Bluefield State College.)

A few weeks after submitting his application, Jacob received a call from Mrs. Blankenship, a secretary at Bluefield Colored Institute, to come in for an interview the following Friday at 4:00 PM. For the occasion, Jacob put on his best Sunday blue sports jacket, white shirt, and red tie. Mrs. Blankenship greeted Jacob and directed him to sit in the chair outside the adjoining conference room. After a few moments Principal Hamilton Hatter, a tall thin Negro man with a salt and pepper beard growing out of the sides of his cheeks, like wings of a seagull, appeared and introduced himself. Joining Principal Hatter was the President of the Board of Regents, Nathen Cook Bracket, a white man with an engaging smile. Jacob later learned that Nathan Cook Bracket was an abolitionist, a Free Will Baptist Pastor, and one of the founders of Bluefield Colored Institute. Nathan began by asking Jacob, "Why do you want to come to Bluefield Colored Institute? We are a poor school."

Jacob was ready for this question, replying, "My parents were slaves who escaped to Canada via the compassionate generosity of people along what was called the great Underground Railroad. I want to help Negro students become teachers, to increase the confidence of colored people, as well as to honor our enslaved and brave ancestors, who sacrificed so we could pursue our dreams."

Hamilton and Nathan looked at each other, quietly acknowledging they liked what they were hearing.

Jacob continued, "Like an ember sitting in a campfire waiting for a breeze to burst into flames, I want to give students that lift, the breeze, by which they will develop a life passion to learn long after they leave here."

Hamilton asked Jacob to step outside, and then he said to Nathan, "I like Jacob's energy, values, and education philosophy; his parents' struggles have strengthened his will to give back to colored people and raise the confidence and knowledge of his students. We should hire him now!"

Jacob went on to teach at Bluefield Colored Institute for many years. There he met his future wife Betsy, a student who graduated with a degree in English. Betsy, after graduation and marriage, worked as a reporter at the Bluefield Daily Telegraph. One of her first major articles was about the coal boom in West Virginia, bringing to light how coal contributed to the State's population diversity. Europeans and Negros came to West Virginia to mine coal, which increasingly was used to power locomotives and run factories throughout the United States. Betsy humanized her stories by describing the luxurious houses of the West Virginia coal barons, many of whom lived in the Bluefield area. She mentioned how the Bailey and Davidson families had sold portions of their land to Captain John Fields of the Norfolk and Western Railroad. The N&W Railroad, as Betsy wrote in her articles, then made Bluefield their home for its Pocahontas Division because the area's geography allowed natural gravity switching of the coal trains out of the northwestern coal fields.

In another article, Betsy reminded her readers that coal was not the first natural resource that was mined. The first was salt. Before refrigeration, salt was used to preserve food. The Kanawha River Valley had rich underground deposits, which could be mined by injecting water, then pumping out the salty liquid and boiling off the liquid to produce salt. Salt, Betsy informed her readers, was used extensively during the Civil War by both sides. Salt was an essential ingredient - safeguarding the precious food that was providing nutrients for a soldier's body and soul. Betsy added that the Confederacy suffered a major blow when the Union troops captured the salt mines in West Virginia during the Civil War.

After a few years of tranquility with Jacob teaching at Bluefield Colored Institute and Betsy reporting for the Daily Telegraph, it was time to start a family. Firstborn was Ruffas, second Grace, and third Elizabeth. Herman Jackson was born in 1914, as the sweet fragrance of apple trees was blooming at home, and dark ominous clouds were forming across the political landscape in Europe.

Chapter Five

WORLD WAR AND A PANDEMIC

SHORTLY AFTER HERMAN was born, events in Europe exploded into violence. Archduke Franz Ferdinand of Austria and his wife, Sofie, were assassinated by a Bosnian Serb in Sarajevo. World War I began soon thereafter with Austria-Hungary declaring war on Serbia. Then Germany declared war on Russia, France, and Belgium; Britain declared war on Germany; Austria declared war on Russia; Japan declared war on Germany, and Austria declared war on Belgium. Europe was about to be engulfed in flames.

The United States did not enter the war until three years later when it declared war on Germany in 1917. Germany had practiced unrestricted submarine warfare, including sinking ships carrying United States civilians and cargo. The final straw came when a telegram was intercepted and decoded by British intelligence from the German Foreign Secretary, Zimmerman, to the Mexican government. It proposed a war alliance between Germany and Mexico if the United States entered the great war against Germany. Germany was hoping that if the United States became involved in fighting

Mexico, the US would not join Great Britain and France in the war against Germany. The intercepted telegram was one more incentive to those in favor of joining the Allied Powers. The United States mobilized, used propaganda to sell the war effort, drafted troops, and produced the food, equipment, and munitions necessary to win the war. The government enlisted the help of women to work the assembly lines, while Negros were hired to work in department stores for the first time. Liberty gardens sprang up as Americans grew their own food so more produce could be diverted to the troops. American forces fought valiantly. World War I ended when Germany, with its morale collapsing both at home and in the military, surrendered on November 11, 1918.

West Virginia was a major contributor to the war effort. Coal was produced and utilized in factories producing trucks, tanks, and munitions. It was also used for steam engines that transported military goods and troops to ports for dispatch overseas. Negro American men were big participants in coal extraction; Negro women organized canning clubs, sold war bonds, and educated the public on the importance of patriotism. Betsy was active in writing stories about courageous West Virginian men who fought in different battles. She was also active in the Auxiliary Defense Council, whose purpose was to educate the public about how to conserve food and fuel. Her efforts were joined by two colored sisters from Beckley, West Virginia. Ethel and Ada Peters published a book of poems urging colored folks to embrace solidarity with the war effort while dramatizing poetically the discrimination people of African descent faced in the United States. Children too were involved in support of the War. Herman helped his mother in their victory garden, and he was active in the Junior Red Cross.

Not only did Jacob, Betsy, Ruffas, Grace, Elizabeth, and Herman have to cope with World War I, they and their community of colored folks also had to endure a life-threatening flu pandemic. In 1918 the highly infectious and virulent disease had caused illness amongst soldiers in training at Camp Funston in Fort Riley, Kansas. Within weeks cases of the flu spread through the United States, Europe, and Asia as conditions of World War I, overcrowding in barracks and trenches, and global troop movements helped spread the flu. The vulnerability of healthy young adults and the lack of vaccines or treatments created a major global health crisis. The virus that caused the Great Influenza Epidemic would infect 500 million worldwide, one-third of the population on the planet, and kill 50 million, including 675,000 in the United States. The first wave of the flu was relatively mild, but the second wave was even more contagious and deadly. The flu was often referred to as the Spanish Flu, but it did not originate there. During WWI Spain was a neutral country, and its news media reported on the devastating effects of the flu. Other countries, not wanting to appear weak, banned reporting of the flu pandemic. Thus, it was called the Spanish Flu because more news about the flu was coming out of Spain.

In Chicago and other cities throughout the United States movie theaters and night schools were closed. Large public gatherings were discouraged. Other preventative measures were employed. The San Francisco Board of Public Health required anyone serving the public to wear masks. At least three waves of the virus, each more deadly than the last one, were to attack the United States population. The virus was unique in that it most seriously affected relatively healthy adults, including US servicemen, resulting in more soldiers dying from the 1918 flu than were killed in battle.

In Bluefield and the surrounding area of Southern West Virginia, the flu wiped out entire families, leaving widows, widowers, and orphans. The flu depressed the economy as businesses were shut down. Schools like Bluefield Colored Institute closed for a while; coal production decreased as miners fell ill, and basic services such as mail delivery and garbage collection were adversely affected.

Jacob took the lead, informing his students of the need to take precautionary measures like wearing face masks, keeping safe distances from other students, washing hands, and avoiding touching one's face. Jacob knew the devastating effects the flu could have on a family.

Later in the pandemic, Jacob used the event as a case study of missteps taken and lessons learned. Jacob informed his students, "Nationally there was a lack of leadership to identify the problem, quarantine those stricken with the flu, and promulgate tried and true measures that worked in the past during other pandemics, like avoiding large gatherings and wearing face masks. In 1918, doctors and scientists did not know what the cause of the flu was. Officials estimated that the pandemic would go away soon and suggested wrong treatments like giving toxic doses of aspirin. Public health was almost non-existent in many areas. Many citizens refused the advice of experts and downplayed the severity of the pandemic for their own selfish economic and personal interests. Public health officers, governors, mayors, and our national government failed to act swiftly because they did not want to be seen to be unpatriotic during wartime or against big business or workers who need a paycheck to feed their families."

"But wait a minute," a student said, waving his arm to speak, "didn't our government have experience with other diseases that spread quickly?"

"Yes," Jacob replied, eager to get his students involved. "Developments in public health successfully tackled cholera, typhoid fever, and diphtheria, which were deadly, but were managed and later found to be preventable."

"So, what happened as a result of the failures?" another student chewing on a pencil asked.

"Well," Jacob said, "let's look at a few examples. In Philadelphia in September of 1918, when 300 sailors, some of whom were infected already, docked at the Philadelphia Navy Yard, the Director of Public Health, lacking training in infectious disease, insisted that there was nothing to worry about. He never requested additional doctors or nurses in case there were mass hospitalizations. He never quarantined the ship, even though the city was about to have a large parade to support war bonds. As a result, within ten days, one thousand Philadelphians were dead, and before the wave of cases was finally over fifteen thousand residents died."

"Not only were people asked to remain calm by leaders of the Federal and State governments, but there were also plenty of snake oil salesmen, who tried to take advantage of the fear that was gripping the country. 'Take this or that. It is sure to cure you,' they falsely proclaimed. There was also widespread resistance to closures and quarantine because the public received mixed messages about the severity of the pandemic." Jacob added.

"Why does the pandemic affect people differently?" a student asked.

"Usually during an epidemic people who are poor and live in unhealthy conditions are more likely to have higher rates of morbidity and mortality. So, it was not unusual that at first, the media reported that people of color were more likely to get the virus and die. That misinformation caused persons of African descent to be stigmatized as unclean or carriers of the deadly pathogen. This, however, later turned out to be false. Reported cases showed that colored folks were less likely than the White population to be infected by the Spanish Flu, but more likely to die from it once they developed the disease," Jacob responded.

The case study was well received. As the students left the classroom that day, they were quiet. There was not the usual chatter about what was happening that weekend. It had stopped raining outside. The sun was breaking through puffy clouds, sending slivers of light through classroom windows. The students had absorbed a lesson learned.

Jacob Jackson had always wanted to work at the university level. In 1919 he got his chance. He answered an advertisement, and sent in his resume to John Smith University, a college in Charlotte, North Carolina, established in 1867 for descendants of Africans. Several weeks later Jacob received a phone call from a registrar at John Smith University. They would like for him to teach US History to freshmen. Jacob and Betsy were excited to be moving to Charlotte, a city so named by King George III after his wife, Queen Charlotte.

The Jackson family settled in the Brooklyn community in the Second Ward in downtown Charlotte. It was a depressed area that was lower than the other four wards of Charlotte, which sometimes caused flooding and sanitary problems. Many of the emancipated slaves had settled there. Gradually it became a thriving black business center with its first public school.

The Jacksons moved into a six-room house with a wood stove in the kitchen, an old table where they ate their meals, a bedroom for Jacob and Betsy, as well as one for Herman and his brother Ruffas. There was another bedroom for his sisters Elizabeth and Grace. Because Jacob's parents, John, and Loretta, had limited funds, Jacob constructed a staircase and put a bed for them in the attic. They stretched their tight budget by buying clothes at the Salvation Army and cooking vegetables that Betsy and Loretta gathered from their backyard garden as well as the farmer's market.

Jacob was assigned to teach United States History at John Smith University, in the northern end of Charlotte. Jacob liked history, especially the Revolutionary War and the War of 1812. For the Civil War, he tried to show that the South had an agrarian culture that was not fully understood by people in the North. When questioned about slavery one day Jacob responded factually without giving his opinion, "My father was a slave near Charlotte and escaped to Canada before returning to America to live in West Virginia."

Chapter Six

HERMAN JACKSON'S
SCHOOL YEARS

I N THE MYERS Street School in Charlotte, Jacob and Betsy's son Herman sat in the front of the class, and he was usually the first to raise his hand with an answer or a question. Herman did not try to play tricks or talk to draw attention to himself when the teacher's back was turned like some of his classmates. He was perceptive and sensitive at an early age. One of his classmates, Benjamin, had a speech impediment which caused him to stutter. Herman stepped in when other students made fun of Benjamin.

"It is not Ben's fault that he talks the way God made him," Herman would say.

The school was segregated and cramped, as were most things in the Brooklyn section of Charlotte. Teachers had to instruct students in two grades per classroom, often with outdated textbooks that were sent over from other school districts where white students went to school. The Myers Street School building looked like it could use a good cleaning and some fresh paint. The toilets were often backed up. The school, like all of Brooklyn, was in a low-lying area making the normal flow of sewage difficult. Herman, always eager to learn, did not let his surroundings bother him.

When Herman was in the first grade, school became much less important and rewarding for a time, as Herman's world, collided with the racial medical discrimination against colored folks, particularly with the medically insufficient treatment of his grandfather. Herman was close to his grandfather, John, affectionately known by all as Pappy, who, along with his grandmother Loretta, whose nickname was Mabel, lived with them because of the difficulty in maintaining separate living arrangements. Pappy had just turned 76 years old, and time had slowed him down. He was a good listener who liked to engage in long conversations with Herman while they were fishing or gathering berries. He had a great deal of patience in answering all of Herman's questions about why the colored people living in the Third Ward had so few creature comforts compared to the White people living across town. Pappy would redirect Herman's concerns from what they did not have to what they did have. They had a wonderful family, people who cared for each other, and freedom. Herman liked to hear his grandfather's stories about growing up on the White Oak Plantation. One day, as his grandfather related how he and his grandmother escaped and ran in the rain at night through a swampy area, Pappy began to cough, louder and louder. Herman watched as sweat formed slowly on Pappy's forehead and his breathing grew shallow.

"I think I need to lie down," Pappy said, looking tired and not well. He slept for about 12 hours, waking up in a cold sweat. He had a fever and complained to Loretta that his body ached all over.

Herman kept asking his mother, "What's the matter with Pappy?"

"I am not sure. He may have the virus. I will call Doctor Reynolds, and see if he will come over," his mother replied.

Doctor Marvin Reynolds was a big, barrel-chested man of African descent with black salt and pepper hair and a full beard. His father had been a slave and then a sharecropper. His mother was the daughter of a Native American woman and a White South Carolinian planter. She was called by the populace a half-breed. She had worked as a maid for a physician, Doctor Wilson in

Bluefield, West Virginia. Doctor Reynolds, as a young boy, often accompanied his mother to the family home and medical office of the Wilson family. It was there while observing patients in the waiting room of Doctor Wilson, that young Marvin felt the pull toward the needs of others. Marvin's dad wanted Marvin to help him on the farm as a sharecropper, which required no further education. His dad thought education was filling Marvin's mind with worthless knowledge. Marvin and his mother saw a different path, which would lead Marvin to Meharry Medical School and then to becoming a family doctor. Meharry originally functioned as the Medical Department of the Central Tennessee College in Nashville. Then it became one of the first medical schools dedicated to training Negro students to be doctors.

When Doctor Reynolds examined Pappy, Herman's grandfather was coughing, had a fever, and had difficulty breathing. After listening to his chest, Doctor Reynolds noted that Pappy had fluid in his lungs. Dr. Reynolds took his stethoscope out of his ears and said softly to Jacob, Betsy, and Loretta, "I am sorry, but Pappy has the Spanish Flu. I suggest you bring him to Good Samaritan Hospital. He needs to be admitted. If his respiratory condition gets worse, he may come down with pneumonia, which can be life-threatening at his age."

Jacob wasted no time in putting Pappy into his horse carriage to bring him to Good Samaritan Hospital. Betsy and Loretta stayed behind with Herman, Ruffas, Elizabeth, and Grace. What Jacob saw when he arrived at the hospital looked like a war zone. Patients with just mild injuries or no severe symptoms were sent home, while others, coughing, with high temperatures, some with bodily fluid oozing out of their noses, screaming uncontrollable delirium utterances, and diagnosed with the Spanish Flu, were separated until they could be admitted to a ward where patients were quarantined. Worried family members were asked to leave the immediate area after giving information to the clerk who was frantically trying to keep track of everyone. The harried look on the nurses going from patient to patient added to the distressful scene. The chaos of the emergency treatment area was shadowed by an ominous feeling, as if Death was walking slowly, like an amorphous black cloud accompanied by far-off rolling thunder, carefully selecting his next victim.

After what seemed like an eternity, Jacob was informed by a nurse who was of African descent like most of the staff, that all the beds were filled. Pappy's symptoms were not as severe as those of other patients, so it would be best if his dad was cared for at home.

"What? Can't you see how sick he is?" Jacob pleaded, red-faced with wet eyes.

"I am sorry. This flu is highly contagious. Your dad and you are better off not being around these more severe flu patients," the nurse added as a doctor was calling her away.

"What about Saint Peter's Hospital?

"They do not take us colored folks."

With the help of an orderly Jacob was able to put his father into his carriage and head home. Upon arriving they were greeted by the concerned look of Loretta and Betsy and the rest of the family. Herman followed his father as they put Pappy in a bed, they had made up for him in their living room. Throughout the next few days, Herman listened as the grandfather's coughing and breathing grew worse, and he went in and out of consciousness. Herman, although a young boy, did not want to leave him alone. Herman opened the windows to let fresh air in, brought water, and put a cold moist cloth on Pappy's forehead to comfort him. Herman's routine actions, taken out of love, left a mark on him that was destined to change his life forever. Finally, with curtains waving from a gentle breeze coming from an open window, Death walked into the room. He did not want the man who had suffered from an overseer's whip, struggling to gain freedom by running, and always searching for acceptance to feel any more pain. So, Death took Pappy peacefully away. Outside a wren, perched on a branch of a sweet-smelling magnolia, welcomed the warm rays of the sun breaking through soft heavenly clouds.

High School Years – A Quest for Knowledge and Speed

After eight years Herman moved on to the Second Ward High School. In 1923, Charlotte had built two high schools: Central High School on Elizabeth Avenue for White students and the Second Ward High School on Alexandria Street for Black students. Herman excelled as a student and as an athlete, particularly in track. In biology class, by learning and memorizing all the bones, muscles, and organs that occupy the human body, Herman impressed his teacher, Mrs. Dominick, an older Negro woman who wore her hair in traditional African braids. He enjoyed using an old microscope, which allowed him to see creatures like amoebae and small larvae. Mrs. Dominick asked Herman to lead the students in dissecting a frog in the biology lab, hoping that his passion for learning would spill over to the others, the way ripples form and disburse when a rock is thrown into a lake.

✧ ✧ ✧

Track coach TJ, short for Tommy Jason Riley, was a former track star at The University of North Carolina at Chapel Hill. TJ would have gone to the Olympics if he had not sprained his ankle before the trials. During Herman's freshman year TJ spotted Herman running a race against a classmate in gym class. TJ noticed that Herman had a smooth effortless stride. Although competitive at short distances, TJ thought Herman would excel more at longer distances like the quarter or half-mile. Herman took TJ's advice, joined the track team, absorbed TJ's instructions, and devoted himself to training, rising early and running miles before class. He would not let himself be late for school. Running for Herman was in his blood. Both his parents were quick although they had little opportunity to compete. Heman liked the feeling of the wind on his face when he ran, but mostly he wanted to be as fast as he could to honor those like his grandfather who ran to freedom. Running allowed Herman to shed his doubts, reach new milestones, and gain confidence. Nurturing his self-esteem which was constantly under stress from prejudice.

TJ was anxious to see how Herman would do in a meet against older boys.

On a day when the wind was bending trees at Charlotte's Central High School, Jacob and Betsy were in the stands looking down at the quarter-mile track that surrounded the school's football field. Jacob looked around and saw the Caucasian parents, well dressed with a polished look on their faces, a persona that mirrored the fine athletic facilities of the school their children attended. Herman was to run the half-mile. The runners took their mark, and the starter sent them flying around the oval track with a loud crack of his gun.

Herman was nervous and anxious, resembling the feeling he experienced when he first asked a girl to dance at a church social. Herman, on the inside lane, could not tell how far he was off the pace because of the staggered start. When the runners converged, Herman realized to his amazement that five runners were ahead of him. As they entered the next turn in the oval, a tall lanky, runner from Central High passed him so close their elbows collided. Breathing hard, the competitor gave Herman a warning, "Watch it, boy! Coming through!"

At that moment, Herman's jitters left him like a sneeze. Gritting his teeth, he shifted into another gear, and let his legs find their own natural, smooth rhythm. He felt the wind warm upon his face. As he passed one of the runners, a sense of freedom filled his lungs. He gulped the crisp spring air. Determination was building inside of him, like a fire escaping its smoldering embers. Herman passed another runner. With 200 yards to go three runners were ahead of him, including the one with whom he had locked elbows. Entering the straightaway everyone was giving it all they could; veins on their necks were bulging, and sweat was pouring off their foreheads. Herman, inspired by a can-do attitude branded into him by his grandfather, came in second, as he passed two more runners at the finish line, including the tall skinny one.

Catching his breath Herman looked up and saw his parents in the stands clapping. Herman felt good that he did well against older students, overcoming the tension of running a longer distance, and being slighted by a White kid. It was one of many hurdles Herman would clear.

✧   ✧   ✧

Herman continued to excel in his studies, a fact that made his classmates uncomfortable due to their own shortcomings. He was often bullied by older, bigger students, like Larry Beam, who had broad shoulders, and was thick around the neck, with dark piercing eyes like a guard dog. Larry was protective of his sister, Abigail. He suspected that Herman's intentions toward his sister were bad, even though she was no more than Herman's biology lab partner. Larry, presuming that Herman was going to mistreat his sister, went out of his way to belittle, or nudge him in the hallways. One day outside school Larry was with two of his buddies, Ricky Davidson, and Travis Crawford. Larry put his shoulder into Herman's back with such force Herman fell to the ground. Larry had not been satisfied with just disrespecting Herman. It was clear that they wanted to give Herman a beating. Herman did not let Larry get into his head. He recalled stories of his grandfather: *experiencing humiliation and whipping by the overseer of the White Oak Plantation, protecting women there like his grandmother, Loretta, running away with her by way of the Underground Railroad. Next to those hardships, Larry is a minor ailment, a bee sting, that after the initial pain would soon be forgotten.*

Herman stood up, looked down at his ripped pants torn at the knees, and shouted, "What the hell did you do that for?"

Larry responded, "Because I do not want you hanging out and screwing my sister."

Herman, feeling the pain in his back, barked, "Abigail and I are just classmates. Not that it is any of your damn business."

Larry answered by throwing a punch that caught Herman on his forearm that was raised quickly in defense. As Herman tried to get out of the way of the second blow, he heard Ricky and Travis yell, "Get him, Larry." The ground rose to meet Herman as blows rained down upon him. This was repeated again and again. Spitting out the dirt after his third trip down, rising slowly, Herman, thought about his grandfather again: *his grit, courage - risking death to shelter those he cared about from oppression, helping his grandmother run to avoid the indignity of rape by the plantation's overseer.* Herman was filled with the strength of righteousness. Herman then flung dirt he had picked off the ground into Larry's eyes, followed by a kick to his groin and two punches to his head.

As Larry fell to one knee, Herman quickly placed his arm under Larry's chin, cutting off his air in a powerful headlock, and screamed, "I am the grandson of a noble slave, who stood up to plantation overlords. I will not be bullied by you. Do you understand?"

Herman loosened his chokehold enough for Larry to respond while gasping, "Yah, Yah, I get it." Herman turned and faced Travis and Ricky with his hands clenched into fists and his eyes so fierce they backed away and let Herman pass.

This was not the only occasion when Herman used his love of his family, recalling images of his grandparents' past struggles, to overcome his own difficulties. Herman's father, also remembering and teaching the lessons of Pappy's life, often said to Herman, "In the forest, the trees that grow the tallest are the ones that must fight for their sunlight; whereas in the meadow, with plenty of sunlight, a bush barely grows above waist-high." With such advice, Herman continued to grow.

Chapter Seven

HERMAN GRADUATES FROM HIGH SCHOOL

BEFORE GRADUATION FROM Second Ward High School, Herman began to think about going to college. There were not many choices for African American boys. Most private schools were hard to get into. After considering his options, Herman decided to go to John Smith University, a segregated college where his father was a professor. There was a culture there of freedom to learn in the classroom and from each other without fear of prejudices handed down from one generation to the next.

Since his dad worked at the University, Herman felt he might get a break from the tuition. Still, it would be difficult as his family had little money to spare. Growing up Herman, Ruffas, Elizabeth, and Grace often had to pick sweet potatoes or strawberries on neighboring farms to get extra money and food for their family. Many times, a family meal consisted of what was brought home to make a stew. Herman in high school already had a part-time job in the University Library stacking books and cleaning the biology and chemistry labs. Maybe he could get a scholarship or run track or go out for football. Herman walked over to the stadium one day feeling the cinders of the track crunch underneath his feet. As Herman looked over the football field, closing his eyes, *he could hear the roar of the crowd as he received a punt, dodged left, faked right, and made his way into the end zone. In high school, TJ had motivated him to excel in track, but in college maybe it was time to change sports. Yes,* he thought, *there were endless possibilities, all that was needed was the will to seize them. Smiling, he pictured a hawk swooping down to grab a field mouse.*

Herman knew that Johnson Smith University was interested in increasing its notoriety, and therefore football would open more doors to a partial scholarship than track. So, one day Herman went over to the University to talk to the football coach, Felix Wilson. Herman rode his bicycle through his Brooklyn neighborhood in Charlotte towards Johnson Smith University. Brooklyn was a booming area for the colored community with its professional class and commercial district, which was often called the Harlem of the South for its music, food, and culture. Sure, there were slums and poor families in Brooklyn, but there were also fine homes inhabited by middle-class colored families as well as scores of black churches, black-owned businesses, restaurants, nightclubs, and movie theaters like Savoy's. Originally, after the Civil War and reconstruction, Negro families settled throughout Charlotte's four wards, living side by side with White families. Then when segregation took hold of the South from the 1890s on, people of African heritage lived in and developed booming areas like Brooklyn within cities like Charlotte. He rode past the Brevard Street Library. It was the first free library for Negros in North Carolina, built after the Carnegie Library in Charlotte refused to admit patrons of color. Herman rode past pushcarts full of vegetables, waving to familiar faces like Mr. Bailey who was stacking tomatoes. Then he went by the YMCA, followed by the AME ZION Publishing Company, which his father said was one of the first Negro owned businesses where people of color could learn a White man's profession. Further down on Brevard Street he passed the Mecklenburg Investment Company, which

64

his dad had told him was financed by people from Brooklyn to serve as a place where the black professional class could prosper. Around the corner, Herman passed Moe's, where his mother shopped for groceries. She had the freedom of knowing that if her bill was more than what she had, Moe would put the remainder on her tab.

Like a deer trying to catch a distant scent, Herman raised his head slightly to take in the smell of a heap of fresh bread coming from a neighborhood bakery. Smiling, Herman felt a sense of pride, being part of a larger family, a camaraderie that only comes in places where business owners know your name, extend credit, and take time to ask how you are or a family member is doing. Moe, for instance, would ask his Mother at check out, "How does Jacob like his job at John Smith University? Yesum those college kids are fortunate to have a professor like Jacob." Or when Herman went with his dad to the hardware store, a question from old Elmer might be, "Hey Herman, how fast did you run the last race against those pups at Central High? Did they get a gander of your backside as you crossed the finish line?" Herman thought *the shopkeepers and people of Brooklyn did not have much, but what they had was trust in each other, like knowing water would flow when you turn the faucet. The anxiety that sets upon some folks, who are worried when a neighbor has more things, did not visit them – for they were in it together, knowing they would rise like a popover if they took care of each other.*

Upon arriving at Johnson C. Smith University Herman was impressed by the campus and the look of well-being among the students sitting on the grass in the courtyard.

"Where can I find Felix, the football coach," he asked one of the students lying on the lawn and looking up from a book he was reading.

"Over there in his office at the field house. Turn right after the big elm tree and follow the path. You cannot miss it," replied the student.

Herman followed his instructions to the field house. He then knocked on the door with "Coach Felix Wilson" painted in big black letters on its frosty window.

"Come in," a deep hoarse voice behind the door proclaimed. As Herman entered Coach Felix stood up. He was a colored man who had big brown eyes, a receding hairline, a jaw with angles that resembled the bottom of a stop sign, broad shoulders, a barrel chest, and hips that looked like he could win a tug of war with a plow mule. His attire was sparse, a pair of shorts, a sweatshirt, long white stained socks, and football shoes.

"Coach Wilson, I'm a senior at Second Ward High School, and I'm interested in playing football with your team," Herman proclaimed, his voice shaking as if he was reading something formal from the Bible.

"Sit down son, I am sorry, I did not get your name? Do you play football now in high school?"

"No Coach, I run fast. My father, Jacob Jackson, who teaches here at Johnson Smith University thought it best that I stick to track. I run the quarter and half-mile, but I am faster than anyone at our school in a 50-yard dash. My time in the 100 is 10.9," Herman said, not boasting, just stating facts.

As he arranged papers on his oak desk containing offensive plays, Felix asked, "So what makes you think you would be good at football?"

"Running away from a foe is something I inherited from my grandfather.

So, avoiding being tackled and outrunning my opponents is in my blood."

Felix stopped shuffling papers, looked at Herman, and leaned forward.

"Your grandfather seems to be an inspiration to you. Tell me about him?"

"My grandfather, John Jackson, who we called Pappy, was a slave at the White Oak Plantation, not far from here. The colored folks respected him because he opposed the overseer's treatment of the female slaves. Pappy suffered the lash repeatedly because of it. Finally, he ran away to Canada. Pappy escaped with one of the slaves, who later became my grandmother, Loretta, who we call Mabel. They had the support of many people and returned to the States after the Civil War. Football will give me the chance to relive my grandfather's struggles, and it will be an atonement for the wrongs visited upon him as well as a window to my own freedom."

"Freedom? Not sure I follow you," Coach pressed for an answer.

"Freedom from being put down because of the color of my skin or where my descendants originated. My accomplishments on the field will eclipse any notion of what I do not have by what I do have. Give me a chance Coach, and I will make you and the 'Golden Bulls' proud," Herman proclaimed like a general leading his troops into battle.

"Well son, you certainly are motivated, and we could use your speed," Felix said, with his mind thinking of a referee holding up both arms to the roar of the fans.

"One more thing," Herman interrupted as he reached out to shake Felix's hand. "I really cannot afford the full tuition here. Is there any way I can get some scholarship money?"

Smiling Felix grabbed Herman's outstretched hand and said, "Ain't you the bold one. Never played football and yet you're sure you will be a star. Now you're asking for moola. I tell you what, if you play as good as you think you can, I will recommend a partial scholarship that will begin with the start of your second semester."

"Sounds good," Herman responded as he gave Felix a firm handshake.

Herman couldn't wait to tell his parents. He was going to Johnson Smith University, majoring in pre-med and playing football. He felt that having clear goals made life easier. To get ready for his switch to football, he decided to concentrate on running shorter races, although coach TJ Riley wanted him to run the mile or a five miler. Herman was stubborn. Running a mile or a five-miler was not going to pay for any tuition.

At the next meet, Herman was scheduled to run a quarter-mile to see how he would do at a shorter distance. Herman decided to go all out from the gun blast to the finish. As he got ready at the starting line, he let his thoughts drift *to images of mad dogs, foaming at their mouths, chasing his grandparents through a swamp.* Propelled by that picture, Herman on the second lane beat the other runners with room to spare.

Two weeks later there was the Statewide High School Track Meet. This was real competition, and Herman convinced Coach Riley to let him try the two-hundred-yard sprint. On the race day, Herman rode with Coach TJ to Central High School, where the state meet was being held. Herman was tapping his hands on the van's dashboard, like a drummer at an ever-increasing pace. Some of the rest of the track team riding with them were resting their eyes.

Coach Riley asked, "Sleep alright Herman?"

"Nah, never ran a two hundred dash before, so I kept running it over in my head," Herman replied.

"You will do all right. Just look straight ahead. Come out of the blocks with your head up high and push for the finish line. It will be over before you know it," TJ proclaimed.

The two-hundred-yard dash was second on the schedule. After a semifinal heat in which he placed second, Herman was ready for the final. Coach Riley informed Herman that the top runner in the state was running on the outside lane. Herman smiled, displaying determination. He tried to get into his routine: stretching, shaking off the tightness in both legs, and calming his nerves. He was wishing he could still be tapping on Riley's dashboard. He looked at the field of runners who were quietly adjusting their starting blocks, as their parents yelled their encouragement from the bleachers. Herman's father and mother were working, so he did not hear their familiar voices.

Yet there was something he heard. At first, the sound was faint, in the back of his mind, the sound of branches bending, leaves shaking, water in a swamp lapping against trees, and then crows squawking, scattering like buckshot to announce something ominous was coming. Herman tried to concentrate, fidgeting with his starting blocks, but the sounds and mental images grew more intense. *He felt he was having an out-of-the-body experience, like living in his own movie based on his grandparent's history. He could see himself*

68

now sloshing through the swamp, hearing rolling thunder, louder and louder, along with the bark of hounds. Quickly Herman put his feet against the starting blocks. As the gun went off, he hurled himself forward. With his head high and his arms pumping hard like the pistons of a race car.

Initially, he was awkward, off the pace, but halfway through the race, Herman's heart pulsating rapidly, feeling like he was being chased while running for freedom, Herman shifted gears, catching his smooth stride, and he passed two runners and charged forward. Leaning so hard at the finish line, he stumbled forward as the ground rose to meet his face. When he was pulled up to his feet, like a rag doll with no resistance, Herman collapsed again!

Coach Riley put his arms around Herman saying, "I do not believe it. You came in second at your first two-hundred-yard race. Not bad against the top competitor in the state," he added.

✧   ✧   ✧

Herman was accepted at Johnson Smith University. His parents were relieved that there was the possibility that he might receive a partial scholarship for playing football. A few months later in June, Herman found himself seated with his high school senior classmates in front of a makeshift stage where graduates were to receive their diplomas. It was a solemn occasion, as many of the seniors were the first in their families to graduate high school. Students were dressed as if they were going to services at the Friendship Missionary Baptist Church on Easter Sunday. The women had flowery dresses as well as big hats and the men had jackets and ties. There was a general air of excitement as the commencement speaker, Principal Jefferson Grigsby, noted for his oratory and support for education, greeted the graduates.

Mr. Grigsby stood tall, wore a dark suit, had gray hair, and a beard closely cropped. He began,

> "To the Second Ward High School class of
> 1932, proud family members, and teachers, I

stand before you humbled by the sight of so many accomplished young men and women who have completed their studies and matured into adulthood. Your graduating students have developed lasting relationships, and are now ready to enter a struggle, not only to reach your highest potential as citizens, but also to advance the opportunities, promise, culture, and justice of your race as proud African Americans. Just as you endured the hard work of your studies and athletic competition, you will face other obstacles on your journey. Remember well this day, this place, the friendships you forged, and step up to the challenge. Never falter or accept that you are less than who you are. You are all God's children, equal in his eyes. Draw strength from those who care about you. The strength you will need. Strength your ancestors had when they were forced into bondage and came here. The strength that your great-grandparents or grandparents had when they endured the humiliation of slavery. Feel what they experienced and draw strength from all of it."

As Mr. Grigsby concluded his remarks, you could see smiles on the faces of the parents. Students sat in their seats, eyes focused ahead, while mothers took out their handkerchiefs to dot their watery eyes. When the ceremony was over, graduates experienced a crescendo of emotion, hugs, kisses, and pats on their backs. It was a memory they were never to forget. Like steel forged from iron ore, they were toughened and inspired by the occasion.

Chapter Eight

COLLEGE LIFE AND THE
LAUNCHING OF THE ROCKET

T WAS A hot steamy summer day in August when Herman showed up for football practice with an extra bounce in his step. The athletic resources at Johnson Smith University were sparse compared to other colleges like Duke or North Carolina State, but the enthusiasm was high amongst the Negro football athletes. They had something to prove that was less dependent upon the weights in the training room or the number of seats in their stadium. Herman ran over to Coach Felix Wilson who was standing like a general surveying the strength of his army.

"Hi Coach," Herman said with his hands on his hips.

"Good day, Son. Let's see, your name is Hercules, no it's Herman. I am counting on you. We need someone fast on our special teams, running back punts and kickoffs. I was counting on Jason Marshall coming back, but he injured his knee in a bicycle accident. He will be out for the season. The good thing is you don't need to know our set plays to be successful running back kickoffs."

"Why?" Herman asked.

"Well, it is simple. You catch the ball, hold it tight, then run like hell. Important thing is, when you are hit, do not fumble the ball. Now go to the locker room and let Jimmy Jones, our equipment manager, get you all geared up."

Herman thanked the Coach and headed to find Jimmy. Still rattling around in his head were the coach's words of concern, *when you are hit, do not fumble. Maybe,* he thought, *I should stick to track. At least they do not hit track athletes.*

Jimmy was a short colored man, with a big potbelly, a goatee, and a shaved head that looked like a black cue ball. He warmly greeted Herman, "Welcome aboard. Heard you ran track and will be our key man on our special team. You get hit hard running back punts and kickoffs, so I will make sure you are fitted right. Again, the word "hit" hung in the air, like a dark, ominous cloud, foretelling a calamity yet to happen.

Joining the rest of the team, Herman heard Coach Felix welcome everyone. With a little luck, Coach felt they could make it to the state championships. He asked the new recruits to introduce themselves. Afterward, there was applause giving Herman a warm sense of camaraderie.

Soon September arrived. Herman, eager to start his courses, went to the Registrar to obtain a list of the classes he would take in freshman year. Then he went over to the bookstore, which was in the same brick building, to obtain the textbooks he would need. When Herman saw the high prices of books, he selected second-hand books whenever they were available. Noticing the bill was above his budget, he asked to speak to the manager. After a few minutes, Herman was greeted by a tall thin colored lady, with red-framed glasses, deep red lipstick, and short hair with reddish hints like flickering flames in a campfire.

"Hello, I am Mrs. Dickerson, how may I help you?"

Herman in a sheepish way replied, "My name is Herman Jackson. I am a freshman on a tight budget. I was wondering if you have any jobs at the bookstore, where I could earn enough to pay for my books. I am on the football team, and with football practice, I do not have much time. But I could work in the evening after Coach Felix lets us go."

"Jackson, that name is familiar," Mrs. Dickerson thought out loud.

"My Dad is on the faculty here," Herman said, lifting his head and looking directly at her.

"I hear good things about your dad. His classes are well attended, and he was instrumental in starting the Black History Club that is now spreading awareness of African Americans' achievements throughout our University, Duke, and the University of North Carolina at Charlotte. I am sure your father inspired many students by recalling the histories of our leaders of African American heritage. By attending several meetings of the History Club, I learned a lot about several prominent Blacks with whom I was not familiar. George Washington Carver was one such person. He advanced peanut, sweet potato, and soybean farming, which greatly benefited my native Georgia. There was Lewis Latimer, recognized for inventing the first long-lasting filament for light bulbs. Viola Pettus, a Black nurse, I remember hearing about her compassionate care of patients during the pandemic of 1918, many of whom were members of the Ku Klux Klan. Perhaps the greatest African American who many of the History Club members and I were not aware of was Dr. James McCune Smith. He was an intelligent man who spoke fluent French, German, Greek, Hebrew, Italian, Spanish, and Latin. He was the first Black person to earn a medical degree."

"Wow, he certainly was a smart man. I do not know anything about him"

"Well, your father informed us that Dr. Smith was born a slave in New York City and legally freed when he was 14 years old after New York passed the Emancipation Act in 1827. Despite James's mental aptitude he was denied admission to medical school at Columbia University in New York City because he was Black. He then went to the University of Glasgow in Scotland. He is known for being the first Black physician to debunk medical racism that claimed Africans lived longer and in more comfort in southern states than in states that had abolished slavery. Dr. Smith's research showed that longevity was socially constructed, (due to socioeconomic and living conditions) not biological or geographical factors.

Mrs. Dickson was aware that the struggling economy in Charlotte during what they were now calling the Great Depression, was causing parents of many students to struggle with tuition and living expenses. Soap kitchens at her Baptist Church were stretched. Men gathered on street corners looking for any kind of day labor. Homeless people living in cardboard shacks in parks and in the woods were increasing rapidly in number. The growing poverty cast a long shadow that education institutions like Johnson State University could not ignore. Unable to meet obligations for tuition, students were quietly dropping out. Herman's grit and motivation impressed her.

She grabbed a schedule, pointed her finger at the calendar, and said, "I could use help on Wednesdays and Fridays from 7:00 to 9:00 pm. I will let you take the books now and you can pay me out of your future earnings."

"Thank you, Mrs. Dickerson," Herman said. "See you on Wednesday."

Herman sat in the front row on the very first day of each of his classes and introduced himself to his professors: Miss Howard for English, Mr. Jen Jensen for Mathematics and Calculus, Miss Sanders for Western Civilization, and Mr. Northgate for Biology. Mr. Northgate was particularly interesting when relating the structure and function of living things. Herman was excited when Mr. Northgate mentioned that the class would be spending a great deal of time studying the human body with all its complexity, interconnectivity, and vulnerability. Herman could feel a burning curiosity to learn as much as possible about how the body battles the attack of outside, invisible predators like bacteria and viruses.

With the start of the school year also came Herman's first football game. Herman was thrilled that he made the team, showing in practice that he could take a hit and hold on to the football. Feelings of confidence helped to boost his spirits, allowing Herman to spend long hours practicing, working, going to classes, and studying. The game was with Davidson College in Davidson, North Carolina. Johnson Smith University was part of the Colored Intercollegiate Athletic Association, which was composed of colleges with African American Student-Athletes from Pennsylvania to South Carolina. Not all the school's Johnson Smith played, however, were in the Association. The Davidson Wildcats were in a different conference and a formidable opponent. They had the money to build a first-class football stadium and locker room facility. Johnson Smith University, a segregated Negro college with limited funds, did not have these resources. Along with the larger stadium came Davidson's bigger offensive and defensive line, which towered over the linemen of Johnson Smith University's Golden Bulls. Herman, though, was not concerned about the Wildcat's size. Bulk, especially fat, would make Davidson's players slower and easier to run past.

Being a Saturday at 1:00 pm, a blazing sun was overhead, making the players in uniforms as hot as if summer had returned. Herman looked up in the stands as his father, mother, Ruffas, and Elizabeth were on the 45-yard line about 5 rows up yelling, "Go Golden Bulls!" With the economy in Charlotte and the nation depressed after the collapse of the stock market, sitting in the stands watching their son play in a football game was a luxury for the Jacksons.

After a bit of stretching, Herman heard Coach Felix give his pep talk, and the national anthem was played over the loudspeakers. Herman and each team member stood arrow erect, helmets off, with hands over their chests listening to the recording. Herman's mind wandered. Trying to accept the patriotism of the moment, he had his doubts for he had read: *The Star-Spangled Banner was written by Francis Scott Key, as a poem to commemorate a battle at Fort McHenry during the War of 1812 with Britain. Later it was set to music, and in 1916 it became the national anthem. The War of 1812, occurred when President James Madison, to show his toughness, decided to pursue a campaign against the Indians in the Midwest near the Great Lakes. General William Hull was dispatched to pursue the Indians on the western side of the Great Lakes as they retreated into Canada. The mission then took on a greater goal of "liberating" Canada from the British. Madison and Hall were under the misconception that the Canadians wanted to be free of Great Britain, without realizing that over half of the population were Loyalists that migrated from the thirteen colonies during and after the American Revolution. Hull's army looted farms of Canadians suspected of collaborating with the Indians, resulting in the Canadians vigorously defending their homeland. Hall's army was defeated, and another invasion of Canada was initiated around the eastern area of the Great Lakes. This time American forces burned whole villages, hoping to convince the Canadians by force to support the Americans against the Indians. However, the opposite occurred. Canadians, furious about their treatment by their neighbors to the south, defeated the Americans again. In 1814 the British brought the War to President James Madison's home in Washington DC. They burned down the Capitol Building and the White House. About a month later the British sailed up the Chesapeake Bay to attack Fort McHenry.*

Herman was shocked out of his trance by Coach Wilson, who shouted, "Come on Golden Bulls, let's go get them Wildcats!"

The Golden Bulls kicked off and the game was underway. Having a bigger line, the Davidson Wildcats were able to muscle their way, running the ball up the middle and executing sweeps around the ends for big gains. A five-yard power play plunge sealed their first touchdown.

Coach Felix hit Herman on the helmet, "Now it is your turn to show them what you got."

Herman, feeling lonely all by himself, waited for the kickoff, bouncing up and down on his feet to shake his nervous energy. Finally, after what seemed like an eternity, Herman saw a football coming his way, end over end, high in the air. *"Don't drop it"* and *"don't fumble"* played in his ears. Herman, trying to concentrate, caught the ball on the fifteen-yard line. Immediately running to his right, progressing diagonally ten yards. He spotted a wedge of Wildcats approaching fast, like a giant whale about to swallow him. Herman stopped, reversed direction, and started to run diagonally back, losing ground towards the opposite sideline, where his team was lined up jumping up and down. When Herman was about halfway across, he kicked into another gear, oiled, and steeled from his track days. Flying past his opponents, like a fox being chased by hunting dogs, he made his way up the field near the Golden Bulls' sideline. Finally, an opponent was able to push him out of bounds as Herman crossed the fifty-yard line. Teammates lifted him off the ground. A volcano of emotion overcame him, as Felix yanked him by his facemask and yelled, "Son, that was a hell of a run."

"Sorry Coach! If I had faked that last player out, I could've gone all the way," Herman replied, trying to catch his breath.

"Don't worry, you will. Glad to have you on the Golden Bulls," the coach said, releasing his grip on Herman's facemask while giving him a pat on the back. Herman looked up to the sky in gratitude, feeling acceptance amongst his teammates, who all shared a common purpose along with the color of their skin.

The Wildcats went on to score again, but in the fourth quarter, they were stopped at their thirty-yard line and had to punt. Herman was back receiving the kick, which was high. Momentarily, he lost sight of it in the sun. Herman looked down to clear his eyes when he noticed two Wildcats steaming towards him like a runaway dump truck plummeting down a hill. When they were almost on him, Herman braced for the hit that was sure to come. Instinctively, he looked up, caught the ball on his twenty-five-yard line, faked right, and ran to his left as one of the Wildcats brushed by him. Picking up a blocker, Herman made a cut again, then at midfield, when it looked like three opposing players would take him down, Herman mused: *this one's for you, Pappy - liberty is my end zone.* As if fulfilling a prophecy, Herman ran with amazing speed around the tacklers near his bench. They followed him, like the tail of a kite blowing in the wind, as he crossed the goal line.

The football players, exhausted, left the field as the game came to an end.

Herman walked from the end zone towards the locker room. Raising his eyes he caught a glimpse of his parents in the stands, standing, clapping for a son who was finding his way.

✧   ✧   ✧

Herman had a rigorous academic caseload, which along with football practice and working in the bookstore kept him busy. Any extra time he spent in the bio lab, talking to his biology professor, Howard Northgate, a short Negro man, with broad shoulders, balding, with wire-rimmed glasses. Herman was devouring knowledge which motivated him to ask Professor Northgate endless questions. Professor Northgate one day mentioned to Herman that he had graduated with a degree in biology with good grades intending to become a physician but was not accepted by any medical school.

"Why?" Herman asked.

"Many medical schools felt the segregated colored colleges' premedical academic courses were substandard, so they felt applicants even with excellent grades were not necessarily smart enough, motivated enough, or prepared enough for the difficult world of medical education. With limited enrollment the colored medical schools were hard to get into," Professor Northgate answered with a little resentment in his voice.

"I would like to go to medical school," Herman said, not wanting to be discouraged, and looking like a child playing checkers seeking a secret move that would get him a win.

"One thing I remember from my medical school admission interviews," Professor Northgate said, "was being asked about experiences that made me want to become a physician. My father worked two jobs most of his life to support our large family of seven kids. He shoveled grain for eight hours in the Whitley Grist Mill that produced about 50 barrels of flour a day. Then after a brief nap, he repaired machinery at the Mecklenburg Textile Mill until early evening. We lived in a small rental house with three bedrooms. Any spare time I had, I worked picking tobacco or helping my parents with my brothers and sisters. I could not share any relevant personal medical, scientific, humanitarian, or altruistic experiences during my medical school admission interviews."

It was then that Herman got a lightning bolt of an idea. He would work or volunteer at a nearby hospital, helping to show that he was interested in medicine. It would also help him to understand who the players are on the healthcare team, and how they work together. Herman remembered from when he was a child how his grandfather, Pappy, caught the Spanish Flu. Pappy suffered and died because, among other things, Good Samaritan Hospital did not have enough beds and lacked the latest medical equipment to treat his condition. Herman recalled hearing from his father about patients sitting on the floor coughing uncontrollably due to a shortage of stretchers and witnessing mothers' pleadings with doctors to do something for their children. Making Pappy's experience worse was being discharged from the emergency room with no plan for follow-up care. The memory instilled in Herman a burning desire to ease the medical suffering of colored folks. By volunteering or working in a hospital, he wanted to begin his journey of understanding why people get sick, so he could help them stay well.

Before his English class on Thursday, Herman set out to go to Saint Peter's Hospital seeking employment or a volunteer position to get exposure to the mystique of medicine. At the information desk in the lobby, he asked,

"I would like to inquire about a job." He was directed to go to Personnel. There he met Mrs. Hirsch, a slim lady who looked to be in her late thirties with long blond hair, porcelain skin, glasses covering her big blue eyes, all set in a face with a no-nonsense demeanor. She asked Herman to complete an employment application, and in an authoritative manner, after he returned his completed application, sent him on his way. Walking through the hallways Herman passed by Radiology, Nursing Department, the Operating Room, then unexpectedly he was drawn to the Laboratory. He peered into the frosted glass door marked with black letters "Pathology Lab - John Spenser M.D."

Just then the door opened, and Herman was greeted by a pungent malodorous smell plus a rather large man that would change his life forever.

Chapter Nine

WORKING FOR THE MAVERICK

"CAN I HELP you?" said a welcoming voice from a tall, barrel-chested, large man, with big shoulders, and a salt-pepper beard. He was bent slightly forward, as if he was holding the world up like the mythological Greek god, Atlas.

"Hi, my name is Herman Jackson. I am attending John Smith University, studying biology, and I am interested in pursuing a career in medicine."

"Is that so? My name is John Spencer, but most folks just call me Jake. I am the Director of Pathology and in charge of the Lab. I was about to go to the cafeteria to get something to eat, but, as you can see by my waistline, I have a few extra calories stored. So instead, why don't I show you around the Lab."

"I do not want to impose," Herman said nervously, apologetic, but excited.

"Nonsense, just follow me," Jake commanded, moving forward. After a few steps, he explained, "This is Hematology, where we look at blood cells to see if any are unusual. Over there is our Chemistry area, where we examine the blood for its components, noting variants against standards." Jake pointed to each area in the Lab, waving and greeting the staff as he went. Herman could not help to notice that none of them were dark-skinned like him.

"Next is Histology, where we look at tissues," Jake rattled matter-of-factly.

"Tissues?" Herman repeated, his voice rising as if to ask for more information.

"Yes! Tissues we look at under a microscope tell us the structure of the cells," Jake explained. Herman could tell from his voice that Jake was particularly interested in histology.

"Around the corner, down the hall, with its own entrance, we have the Morgue, where I do autopsies to determine the cause of a patient's death."

"Wow, can I see that area?" Herman asked curiously, aware that his brief tour was getting longer than expected.

"I do not know," Jake said scratching his chin thinking. "I have a cadaver on the table. How is your stomach?"

"Fine, I am a football player for the Golden Bulls. I am used to getting hit," Herman said.

Jake handed Herman a mask to put on, then opened the door and a strong odor invaded Herman's nose. The floor was tiled. A metal table with a blue sheet covered a body. Jake picked up part of the sheet and examined a tag on the patient's toe. "This is Mrs. Goodman, a forty-year-old woman who died unexpectedly, and it is my job to find out why. We are doing some tests, speculating that perhaps she died from a virus or bacteria that attacked her body that caused her organs to fail," Dr. Spencer mentioned officially as if he was talking to a medical student.

"I have studied viruses and bacteria as part of my biology class with Professor Northgate."

"Howard Northgate, I know him from a talk he gave to our Rotary Club about John Smith University and his interest in motivating more Negro students to pursue medicine as a career. He is a good man and would have made a fine doctor if our medical profession was not so prejudicial," Dr. Spencer said.

"I remember when I was a boy my parents made me wear a face mask, because of a pandemic caused by some sort of virus," Herman recalled.

"You're right. More people died than necessary because they did not take seriously the precautions advised by our infectious disease experts to wear face coverings, or maintain social distance," Jake explained.

As they walked out of the Morgue, Herman thanked Dr. Spencer and asked,

> "Do you need any help with cleaning the Morgue or the Lab? You do not have to pay me."

Dr. Spencer thought for a moment: *maybe it is time we hired a person of color, especially one who wants to pursue a career in medicine. Then, instead of what happened to Howard Northgate, who never realized his full potential, we might encourage this student to become a doctor and go on to care for and be an inspiration to his people.*

"Yes, I can use an extra pair of hands, and I will inform Mrs. Hirsh in Personnel to hire you."

After about a week, Herman received a call from Dr. Jake Spence's Office Manager, Mrs. Collins, to come back to the Lab for orientation and to start work.

Reviewing his schedule, Herman said that he could work on Wednesdays from 7:00 a.m. until 9:30 a.m., and Sundays from 10.00 a.m. to 7:00 p.m.

✧ ✧ ✧

Early the next Wednesday morning Herman went to Personnel to complete paperwork registering as a new employee under the watchful eyes of Mrs. Hirsh. She might have looked for a way to disqualify Herman for the laboratory job, because of the way he had approached Doctor Spenser to get his recommendation for employment. Like many of the staff at Saint Peter's

Hospital, however, Mrs. Hirsh knew better than to cross swords with Jake Spenser M.D..

Next, Herman went to see Mrs. Collins. She lowered her reading glasses and held out her hand, "Hi Herman, ready to start?" She had blond hair pulled back in a ponytail, blue eyes, high cheekbones, and an engaging smile.

"Yes," Herman said, still sleepy from studying late the previous night, and still sore from Tuesday's football practice. Mrs. Collins quickly led Herman around the Lab, introducing him to all the Assistant Managers of the Lab's subsections. Herman was impressed by the quiet professionalism of the staff. Dressed in white uniforms, holding clipboards, like worker bees, each focused on the business at hand without any distractions.

"Now Herman, your main job when you come in on Wednesday morning will be to clean, disinfect and sterilize all our glassware, which we use to collect and analyze our blood, tissue, and urine samples. It is important that you know the reasons why you must follow our procedures without any deviation. Bacteria or viruses may be on the surface of these vessels, or on the bench in the Lab. It is essential that they are not transmitted to our staff or contaminate any of our Lab tests. Moreover, when someone has infectious bacteria or virus on their hands and leaves the Lab, they could transmit it to others, as they touch a doorknob or surface in another area of the Hospital. Patients who enter our Hospital do not expect to receive a life-threatening disease while they are under our care. So, failure to follow a procedure that causes an infection to spread is not an option," Mrs. Collins said, looking directly at Herman.

She added in a serious tone, "In order for our medical system to function, patients must trust us. As the Greek physician, Hippocrates proclaimed: *do no harm*. By believing that they will not be harmed, patients come to trust our care for them. It is that trust, Herman, that is the bedrock of our profession. It is the reason people take a prescription for 14 days even though they feel better after 5 days. They do so because they trust what the doctor told them."

Herman received instructions for cleaning and disinfecting, what chemicals to use, and how to put on and take off his protective gear for his work. Mrs. Collins gave him policies as well as articles to read as homework. Herman thought to himself. *This is serious stuff. The way bacteria and viruses could live on the surface of things for days, then emerged like a butterfly from a caterpillar's cocoon, to spread illnesses quickly to unsuspecting human hosts. They are so small you cannot see them, so devious they find a way to replicate, change, adapt, and strike again.*

Herman was fascinated by these creatures, wanting to know as much as possible about them so he could defeat them in the Hospital. He not only devoured everything given to him by Mrs. Collins, but Herman also borrowed books from Doctor Spencer, and read journals in the Hospital's Medical Library. Sitting in a fine burgundy leather chair one day reading the journal *Anthropologie*, Herman suffered the degrading looks of White doctors, who were offended that Herman was invading and threatening their space. *What is he looking at anyway?* they thought. Some even went so far as to complain to the Administration.

When Doctor Spencer found out about it, he confronted the doctors in their lounge, "What are you worried about? That young man is showing an interest in his job that far exceeds what is necessary. He is so meticulous about cleaning and disinfecting the lab, you could eat off my benches. He offered to work for free so he could learn about medicine." Dr. Spencer, red-faced with anger, pushed up the sleeves of his white lab coat from which peaked a Marine tattoo featuring an eagle clutching a Semper Fidelis banner. Then Jake leaned forward, like a mountain lion ready to pounce, and stared down any of his colleagues who might want to utter a condescending word about Herman.

✧ ✧ ✧

Herman excelled in his studies. He received high marks from his professors and appreciation from his classmates for his help with their coursework. Plus, he was recognized beyond Charlotte for his football prowess. Regarding the Golden Bulls, after running back two punts, he was promoted to wide receiver, not just because of his speed, but due to his uncanny ability to leap in the air to catch a football, like he had springs attached to his lower extremities. By senior year, pro scouts were following the Golden Bulls' games to watch the "Rocket," the name his teammates gave him. It seemed certain to fans that Herman was destined to play with the pros. Herman, however, had other ideas.

Chapter Ten

PUBLIC HEALTH AND INFECTIOUS DISEASE

ERMAN WAS ALMOST 5 years old at the time the influenza pandemic of 1918 started to spread in the United States, probably from an army training camp many people thought. Herman realized that he had a strong interest to learn as much as he could about how infections spread amongst people. He remembered the horror of hearing about people dying, seeing people wearing masks, and not wanting to be close to each other. He recalled how the virus suddenly infected his grandfather, Pappy, when he was seventy-six and in good health. How Pappy felt tired, sleeping all the time, gasping for air, and coughing louder and louder. Grandma Mabel and his dad took Pappy to the Good Samaritan Hospital, which was built in 1891 to provide care to Negro families. It was cherished by many in the Black community, but it was not considered to be equal to the other hospitals in Charlotte that treated the White population. Pappy received an evaluation outside the emergency room and then was sent home. The Hospital did not have enough beds, and the nurse suggested it would be better to care for Pappy at home. At the dinner table Herman received daily reports from Grandma as to how Pappy was doing. Then Herman's father would ask the family to bow their heads and join him as he said a prayer.

After struggling as a slave, defending the honor of female slaves, and running away to Canada Grandpa finally took his last breath in 1919, a tragedy that left a lasting impression on Herman, who then wanted to learn as much as possible about infectious diseases. With his good grades at John Smith University, strong references from Doctor John Spencer, and from his biology Professor, Mr. Northgate, Herman applied to several graduate schools. He was accepted by the University of Michigan to study epidemiology and infectious disease. After graduating from John Smith University, Herman spent the summer working with Doctor Spencer in his Lab. In the fall Herman took a train to Detroit, Michigan, and then a bus to the City of Ann Arbor. He was impressed by the size and beauty of the campus. There were about 10,000 undergraduate students enrolled at the university, but only about 15 in his graduate program. The University had many research studies on communicable diseases underway.

After registering for his courses, Herman went to the Epidemiology and Infectious Disease Department to meet the Chairman, Robert Angelus M.D., Ph.D. Herman first knocked and then entered after Mrs. Dahil, the Department's secretary, motioned that it was alright to go in.

"Hello Dr. Angelus," Herman said confidently as he held out his hand.

Dr. Angelus put down some papers, lowered his reading glasses, and shook Herman's hand. His desk was piled high with journals and correspondence. Behind him was a bookshelf filled with books. Dr. Angelus responded "I see, Mr. Jackson, that you are here for a master's degree in Epidemiology with a concentration in Infectious Disease. You came highly recommended by Dr Spencer who is one of our distinguished alumni. How is he?"

"Dr. Spencer is fine. I have learned a lot from him, working in his Lab, cleaning, assisting with autopsies, and just listening to him. He still has a great deal of affection for the Wolverines from his days at the University of Michigan," Herman said with a grin.

"Jake Spencer was an outspoken doctor, a true contrarian; stood up against any mistreatment of his classmates and for equal rights for people of color. During the time he was here Negro students used to sit together in one area of our cafeteria, partly by choice and custom. Jake would sit there and could be heard telling stories," Dr. Angelus said.

"He is the reason I am here. Dr. Spencer spoke highly of your program, and he was instrumental in my obtaining a scholarship," Herman added.

"Is that so, then why not go on and get your Doctorate Degree and do some groundbreaking research?" Dr. Angelus questioned.

"Well, my interest in epidemiology and infectious disease is not only because of the time I spent in Dr. Spencer's Lab but also because my grandfather died of the Spanish Flu. Sure, I want to pursue knowledge in this field, but I also want to apply it and help my people who often suffer disproportionately when an epidemic breaks out. In Pappy's case during the pandemic of 1918 people just died. There were no treatments or vaccines. Being a colored person, he was denied admission to the better, more up-to-date Saint Peter's Hospital. Instead, he was referred to our segregated, ill-equipped, Good Samaritan Hospital in Charlotte," Herman replied leaning forward in his chair.

"I see. Well welcome aboard," Dr. Angelus said as he rose and shook Herman's outstretched hand.

As Herman turned to leave, facing Dr. Angelus, Herman softly spoke, "One more thing, I enjoyed working with Dr. Spencer, and I would love to assist you with any research. You don't have to compensate me, but my scholarship does not cover my living expenses, anything I could earn would be appreciated."

"Thanks, Herman, I will consider it. Always happy to have a motivated student. In this field, it is important to have many perspectives, numerous eyeballs looking at the same problem to stop a communicable disease before it becomes an epidemic or worse, a pandemic. Sometimes someone you don't expect comes up with a solution to an unforeseen problem. You will learn from your studies how Doctor John Snow helped to prevent cholera from spreading when he came up with the novel suggestion to remove a handle from a drinking well.

Herman enjoyed his infectious disease and epidemiology classes at the University of Michigan. He worked and received pay as a Research Assistant for Dr. Angelus, a position that kept him busy.

Occasionally Herman would attend a football game. Their opening game versus Michigan State was especially thrilling, even though the University of Michigan lost 7 to 21. The season was a blowout, as the Wolverines won only one game, against Colombia, all season. Nevertheless, as he sat in the student section among classmates shouting and drinking at the Michigan State game, Herman smiled and drifted off, contemplating what could have been. *If I had gone to a big Division One School instead of the smaller, segregated, John Smith University, would I be on the field instead of watching passively from the bleachers? After a few stellar seasons, I would have been noticed by pro scouts. Would I be famous?* Thoughts lingered in his mind like a butterfly floating in the air. Herman's daydream was interrupted by a fellow student, who, while struggling to get to his seat, spilled some beer on Herman's lap.

Herman did not regret coming to the University of Michigan to obtain his master's degree. He enjoyed his time in Ann Arbor. Before he knew it, graduation was upon him. He had to plan the next stage of his life. Because of his limited funds, Herman knew he could not afford medical school at the time. Since both his parents were teachers, he grew up in a family that embraced education. In view of this, he decided to become a science teacher, until he could save enough money to fulfill his desire to go to medical school.

Chapter Eleven

A NOBLE CAREER

AFTER APPLYING FOR several teaching positions, Herman was accepted to teach biology and serve as an athletic coach at McClelland Academy in Newnan, Georgia, a private parochial school established by the Presbyterian Church. McClelland presented a challenge because there were only 12 teachers for 400 students of African American descent.

Herman enjoyed the camaraderie with his students, teaching them not only about science, but also life lessons and values they would need to overcome the struggles that would surely come their way. A case in point was Willie Night, a senior whose father was jailed. Willie's father had argued with a policeman over why he was on the street. Sometimes all it took if you were of African descent was a perceived bad attitude to get you jailed or beaten.

Herman would say to Willie, "It is important to get your mind right. A bad attitude can get you in big trouble. Think of all the people that love you, and who you love. Drawing strength from love is like retrieving water from a well."

After two years Herman left McClelland Academy when financial problems caused the school to close. Next Herman went to Tuscaloosa, Alabama to accept a teaching position at Stillman College, founded by the Presbyterian Church in 1875 as the Stillman Institute for the training of colored men for the ministry. In 1937, Stillman Institute expanded to include a junior college. Herman taught biology and coached men's basketball. Herman jumped right in, elevating his skills to teach at the junior college level. He enjoyed the curiosity of his students. Many were pursuing two-year associate degrees to work in hospitals as radiology technicians or nurses. A required course for them was biology.

Coaching basketball was another hurdle that Herman confidently cleared. He adopted a strategy of using the speed of his players to press the opposition from the moment the other team took the ball out of bounds. To do this Herman knew he needed to increase his players' endurance. Wind sprints were a critical part of his practices. After the ball came over half court, Herman coached his players to play an aggressive zone or man-to-man defense.

Herman liked Tuscaloosa; a city named after a Muskogean chief. Tuscaloosa had been defeated by the Spanish explorer Hernando de Solo in 1540. Tuscaloosa, the city, was a center of industry and commerce in Alabama, serving as its capital. Tuscaloosa was nicknamed the Druid City after the Celtic group the Druids, who worshiped oaks. Oak trees were planted all over Tuscaloosa's downtown streets. Like Ann Arbor, Michigan, the town was overrun by students. In addition to Stillman Institute, there was the University of Alabama, a football powerhouse that dominated the culture and events of the city.

Herman felt comfortable at Stillman College. It was a beehive of energy. However, one day Herman's world was besieged by an incident that occurred at the Sears Roebuck Department Store. Herman went there to buy some socks. He was walking quickly, as he was pressed for time to get back for basketball practice. He stopped to get a drink of water at the store's drinking fountain.

"What are you doing? Didn't you see the sign?" said a large white man in a police uniform with massive shoulders, arms like the branch of a tree, and a pot-bellied waist.

"What sign?" Herman replied, startled by the question.

"Don't argue with me boy," the policeman barked pointing to a sign that read "Fountain for colored folks." It had an arrow pointing to a black drinking fountain. The one Herman drank out of was painted white.

Herman was indignant. *Why have two fountains and humiliate Negro citizens by ordering them to drink out of a different fountain. Negroes had a different amount of melanin, a pigment that gives skin, hair, as well as eyes their unique color. Herman knew from his study of biology that over many centuries the earliest human populations, who lived close to the equator where the rays of the sun were strongest, evolved through natural selection to have more melanin, causing their skin to be dark as a protective shield against harmful solar radiation. Inhabitants who migrated further north did not need as much protection and probably through the same natural process over centuries came to have less melanin and lighter skin tones. Segregating people for their skin color was no more rational than separating people according to their eye or hair color,* Herman thought.

"Sorry. I did not see the sign," Herman said, conceding that this was not the time to debate the insanity of the practice of separate drinking fountains. Yet the incident left an indelible scar in his subconscious.

After a few years, Herman was ready for a new adventure, so he jumped on a chance to go to Crockett, Texas to teach biology, general science, and be an athletic director at Mary Allen Junior College. The College was founded in 1886, when the Board of Missions for Freedmen of the Presbyterian Church, under the leadership of Rev. Richard Allen, planned for a Black girl's school in Texas. They chose Crockett as the school site because of the area's large Black population. The Reverend Allen's wife, Mary, for whom the school was named, was instrumental in raising funds for the new school. Originally the mission of the school was to offer primary, secondary, and high school education for Negro girls. The school's first President was Dr. J.B. Smith, whose guidance led to the rapid growth of Mary Allen Seminary, the school's original name. During Smith's time, the number of students tripled. But the support for education in East Texas declined after World War I. As a result, the number of students declined. The Reverend Byrd Randall Smith served as the school's first Black President. Under his leadership, the school became co-educational and accredited as a junior college. It was listed as a private denominational junior college with an "A" rating by the Southern Association of Colleges and Secondary Schools.

Crockett, Texas was a town named after Davy Crockett, who reportedly had camped nearby on his way to the Alamo. It was a small town with just a few thousand inhabitants. Although it had none of the excitement, culture, or recreational activities of Tuscaloosa, Alabama, Herman was attracted to Mary Allen College because of the needs of the Negro students and the chance to be an Athletic Director. The school was small and there was no athletic program when Herman arrived, other than field hockey for female students.

Herman enjoyed initiating girls' and boys' basketball programs. He felt that the best way to elevate the standing of colored people was through schooling. Women and men who taught at the Mary Allen facilities could serve as role models, motivating their students and peers to advance through education.

Herman worked at Mary Allen for several years. One day he received a phone call from the principal of his former school, the Second Ward High School in Charlotte, North Carolina. Herman liked Charlotte, and the thought of returning to his old school thrilled him. The school had opened in 1923 when Charlotte built two high schools: Central High for White students and Second Ward High for Black students. Herman was asked to teach biology, replacing Mrs. Dominick who was retiring. Herman would also become the football coach, returning to the sport in which at John Smith University as a Golden Bull he set the school's record for returning punts and kickoffs for touchdowns.

✧　✧　✧

Back Home Charlotte

Jacob and Betsey helped Herman get settled in after his move. It was great to wander through the Brooklyn section of Charlotte and see how vibrant the area had become as a commercial and cultural hub for the Negro population. Herman wasted no time in starting his new job, walking through familiar corridors, past the trophy case, the cafeteria with its memorable comforting smells, and the old gymnasium. In no time Herman settled in, giving positive instructions to his biology students, hoping to inspire them the way Mrs. Dominick had motivated him.

With the football players, Herman was in his element, showing the defensive team how to gang tackle and strip the ball to cause a turnover. On offense, Herman drilled his running backs to protect the football. Repeatedly his backs practiced running through columns of linemen trying to produce a fumble.

It was good to be back in Charlotte. Herman renewed his relationships with neighbors and friends from the old days. One day when Herman was in a laundromat a young lady caught his eye.

"My name is Margarita. I saw you score a touchdown on Thanksgiving Day when you played football for Johnson Smith University," she said smiling. "You ran back a kickoff against Bluefield State College. Going from one side of the field until you changed directions running back to the other side. Then up the sideline. Diving for a touchdown!"

"Oh ya, those players were big and slow, ripe for my signature reverse move," Herman replied factually as if he was merely reporting on the weather. He looked back now at Margarita, noticing that she was tall, slim, with a wide smile accentuated by perfect teeth, curly hair, chocolate smooth skin, and clear brown eyes. The conversation drifted easily about what each was doing since high school, family, and whether they were seeing anyone. They agreed to meet again for coffee, an event that led to a lunch date, and a walk around the shops in uptown. Margarita was an elementary school teacher. She took Herman to her school, proudly introducing him as a teacher and football coach at the Second Ward High School. It was not long before Herman was invited to Margarita's home to meet her parents. When Herman reciprocated by inviting her to meet his parents, Margarita began a lively discussion on the importance of education in childhood development, giving Herman confidence that Margarita was a good addition to his family. A wedding soon followed.

Herman had a big decision to make. Herman was satisfied as an educator, but he always had a calling to become part of the medical field. Herman did not have enough money to pursue a medical career after college. He pursued graduate school at the University of Michigan, and then worked as a teacher, saving money to pay for medical school. When Margarita and Herman's first child, Judith, was born in 1944, she brought great joy to their lives. After taking a semester off from teaching, and arranging for someone to take care of Judith, Margarita resumed teaching. Herman then continued with his plans to go to medical school, the cost of which was possible with their savings, and with some funds from a scholarship he hoped to obtain.

Chapter Twelve

MEDICAL SCHOOL

HERMAN WAS ACCEPTED to go to Meharry Medical College in Nashville, Tennessee. The school was founded in 1875 for the purpose of training Negro doctors, so they would take care of their communities. It was one of six segregated medical institutions established in Tennessee. These medical schools were started after the Civil War when there were few Negro physicians to care for freed slaves. In Tennessee, the environment for colored folks changed from slavery to racial segregation. Legislation and separate but unequal educational opportunities legalized racial discrimination by a collection of State and local Jim Crow laws that lasted from after the Civil War to 1968. The Jim Crow laws took their name from a Black minstrel show character, Jim Crow, often played by actors in blackface. The Jim Crow laws were designed to marginalize people of color by stereotyping African Americans as being lazy or superstitious. The laws were meant to deny Negroes a chance to vote, get a job, and other basic rights like access to healthcare. Most hospitals would not admit

Negroes. Many White physicians, particularly those from former slave states, often would not treat them either.

The Medical College was named for Samuel Meharry, a young Scotch-Irish immigrant, who first worked as a salt trader on the Kentucky Tennessee frontier. Salt was used then as a preservative before refrigeration. In the 1820s, a young Samuel was driving a wagon on a stormy night with wind that was bending trees while rain was blowing sideways. As his horse struggled to pull a load of salt, the wagon slipped off the road into a ditch. The mud, like a giant sinkhole, swallowed the wagon's wheels. Not being able to pull the wagon free, Samuel decided to go into the torrid night and search for help. He saw a small cabin made from logs with swirling smoke coming out of its chimney like it was billowing from the engine of a freight train. As Samuel came closer, through the window he could make out a Negro family who lived there. Recently freed by the master of their plantation, this family was still fearful of bounty hunters, who were paid to kidnap persons of color and sell them back into bondage. Yet this family was about to risk the thing they valued most, their freedom, to give food and shelter to a cold, weary young Samuel that night.

At first light, while it was still raining Clarence Williams and his sons Peter and Silvester pulled Samuel's horse and wagon out of the soupy muck that was swallowing its wheel. The Williams family's simple act of unexpected kindness touched Samuel deeply. Samuel reportedly said, "I have no money to repay you now, but someday when I am able, I will repay your kindness and do something for your race."

Forty years later, after the Civil War ended, and colored folks struggled to gain rights guaranteed by the Constitution, Samuel Meharry was determined to fulfill his promise to the Williams family. When he heard the clergy and laymen of the Methodist faith were organizing the Freedom Aid Society, Samuel and his four brothers pledged $30,000 to support Tennessee's emerging medical education program, and thus repay Clarence's family for their act of kindness. Meharry Medical College's mission to improve the health and healthcare of minority and underserved communities has become widely known. True to its heritage, Meharry Medical College placed emphasis on admitting students of color, particularly those who were poor.

Not being able to live on campus because his funds were limited, Herman, Margarita, and Judith sought housing in Nashville. They found an upstairs loft over a garage on Jefferson Street, which was predominantly an area where Negro families lived and that had become a jazz and blues musical hotspot. Margarita found work at a nearby daycare facility run by a church. Margarita's salary was meager, but she loved the children and the opportunity to use her teaching skills. Herman stretched the family's limited resources by hand washing his clothes every other day. He wore his outfits like they were a uniform. To lower the rent, he negotiated with his landlord, Sidney Grover, to paint the outside of the house and do minor repairs. For food, they ate a lot of rice, beans, and whatever vegetables were in season. Infrequently they bought some inexpensive cuts of meat. Herman had learned the art of cooking with less from his mother, who often made soup, pasta, or vegetable dishes with whatever greens came from the garden. Margarita packed lunches for herself and Herman. She was able to breastfeed Judith during the baby's first two years.

Herman concentrated on his studies at Meharry Medical College with endless determination. Professor of Anatomy, Dr. Mansour, a bent-over large man with a receding hairline and big caterpillar eyebrows, was impressed with Herman's knowledge about anatomy. He was not aware of the many hours Herman had spent with Dr. Jake Spencer working in his Lab and assisting with autopsies. When it came to memorizing parts of the human anatomy, Herman knew every muscle, nerve, vein, and organ by name, and how they functioned. He had a photographic memory and a curious mind, often asking questions that challenged his professors.

Herman's first two years were mostly book learning and labs. His classmates were from disadvantaged Negro families, almost all were their respective family's first generation to be entering the medical field. Herman enjoyed the camaraderie with his fellow students, often trading stories about college or the wars in Europe or the Pacific, where many served after college. Interspersed with stories of glory were the indignities they suffered because of their color.

Herman himself experienced the humiliation of the Jim Crow laws of segregation when he sat down at a lunch counter at Varsallo's Restaurant on Church Street in Nashville. It was about two in the afternoon. There were not many patrons there, so Herman and a fellow medical school classmate, George, who was a little older than Herman, sat down. George served in the Army during the Second World War before going to Meharry. They began talking about Professor Thomas' cytology class, including the amazing things they saw through his microscope. Herman was interrupted by a nudge on his shoulder and a stern barking voice from a gray-haired man with an apron covering his large chest, "What are you boys doing? You know this is where the White folks sit. Your place is over there!"

"What?" Herman questioned looking around, "There is no one else here. Why do you care?"

"Sorry boy," Mr. Big Chest replied, "lions do not eat with tigers. Sometimes separation is for the common good."

Herman, angry, looked over at George who was also fuming. *Hell!* Herman thought. *We are not animals. What difference does it make if persons with different hair or skin color sit together? Maybe it would increase their understanding of each other. If this man was at Dr. Johnson's anatomy class this past Monday when students sliced open their White and Negro cadavers, he would see on the inside we are all the same.* Then a wave of wisdom flushed over their indignation. Herman and George smiled, and rather than moving to the colored section of the lunch area, they stood and walked out in silence.

Several minutes passed without a word being said as they walked along Church Street. There was a gentle breeze rattling leaves as the September sun broke through intermittent clouds. An understanding transmitted between Herman and George, born out of many years of experiencing prejudice.

Like a rock breaking a window, their silence was broken by George, who said in a sympathetic, soft but cracking voice, "Herman, I went to Fisk University right here in Nashville. It was the end of my sophomore year in 1940. In the town of Brownsville,

Tennessee a charter member of the local NAACP, Elbert Williams, was taken from his home by a local sheriff, interrogated, and put in jail. Later Elbert was found by the Hatchie River after he had been lynched. It left an indelible mark on my soul, that was only exceeded by the time I spent in the Army." Wiping the redness in his eyes with his bandana, George slowly continued, "Herman, I fought in the Second World War with the 761 Tank Battalion. We were all colored soldiers fighting valiantly despite the humiliation of not being allowed to fight in battle alongside our White brethren. We were known as the 'Black Panthers.'" George's breathing appeared difficult now, his chest was rising and falling, in the corner of his eyes, Herman noticed moisture. Then George stood with a red face ready to explode as he looked at Herman.

"What's wrong George?" Herman asked.

"They mistreated us," George replied.

"Who? How?" Herman asked, afraid of the answer.

"Everything was segregated in training, mess halls, fighting units, only Black nurses in field hospitals could take care of Black soldiers. We were transported by bus from our barracks to our tank training area. Even though an order proclaimed that the buses were not to be segregated, sometimes White bus drivers still disrespected us. One day our First Lieutenant, Jackie Roosevelt Robinson, was told to sit in the back of a bus by a driver. Jackie was arrested after he refused to comply and stood his ground. He then went through the humiliation of a court-martial, with a charge that he was insubordinate to a superior officer."

"What happened to him?" Herman inquired.

"Jackie was acquitted. Like most Black soldiers, as soon as his time was up, he left the army. I heard that he is now playing baseball and setting records."

"I am impressed. Jackie Robinson clearly was a trailblazer, showing immense courage, standing up for his beliefs and race well before he gained a reputation as an extraordinary baseball player."

"After our training in Fort Hood, Texas, we were shipped to England. We were assigned to General Patton's Third Army. I recall Patton, 'Old Blood and Guts,' speaking to us before we deployed from England. His voice haunts and inspires me to this day. 'Men you are the first Negro tankers ever to fight in the Army. I would never have asked you to join me in battle if you were not good. I have nothing but the best in my Army. I do not care what color you are if you go over there and kill those sons of bitches. Everyone has their eyes on you and is expecting great things. Most of all, your race is looking forward to your success.' Impressive right!"

"Our unit landed on Omaha Beach and saw bloody action in northern France. I saw many tanks of my Black brothers hit, causing soldiers to exit covered in flames. I can still hear their howling screams and smell their burning flesh. Herman, we had to keep going, unable to save them. We later fought in the Battle of the Bulge."

Then George, as they walked along, grew more emotional, sobbed quietly, like a man holding a dying child, tore off his shirt, turned and said,

"Look!" Showing his deforming burns cascaded down his back, like a melting mass of wax. "This is what I must show for my years in combat. No citations, no honor, no thank you, just what some White man told me today, to sit in the colored section of a restaurant." Herman hugged George to console him, two classmates with a bond formed of shared understanding of past wrongs. Their friendship was to last far beyond their study group in medical school.

✧　✧　✧

Nashville

Herman enjoyed his first year at Meharry. Besides impressing Professor Mansour with his knowledge of anatomy, Herman worked hard to master the subjects of biochemistry, histology, and human physiology. He and George often concluded their study group by grabbing a pizza. As they ate one day George described all the material, they had to memorize in their first year, "It is like drinking from a fire hose."

Despite all the hard work, Herman found time to enjoy what Nashville had to offer. One Friday after George and he worked on their cadaver for a while, they left to see why Nashville was called the Athens of the South. Not far from Meharry west of downtown there was a park. They learned that in 1897 Nashville had built an exact replica of the Parthenon. Originally constructed in Athens Greece in the 5th century BC, the Parthenon was the symbol of the power, wealth, and culture of Athens. The one in Nashville was built as part of Tennessee's Centennial Celebration. George and Herman stood in awe looking up at the large statue of Athena in the foyer of the temple. The statue, they read from a plaque, showed Athena, the Greek goddess of wisdom. Herman and George received much of their inspiration to excel in their careers, to give back to their community, from Athena. Hippocrates, a Greek physician considered to be the Father of Medicine, also was influential.

The second year of medical school was devoted academically to the knowledge of pathology, microbiology, pharmacology, and epidemiology. Medical students, working in clinics under the mentorship of residents, also learned how to develop patient relationships. Herman particularly liked immunology and epidemiology. He learned what weakens and strengthens a body to defend itself against protozoa, bacteria, and viruses. He learned that some pathogenic bacteria and all pathologic viruses are intent on invading cells. He could visualize it down to the smallest particle of a cell: its nucleus, cytoplasm, DNA, its proteins. He pictured white cells like honeybees protecting the queen in the hive. Herman spent hours in the lab, looking at different kinds of cells, drawing them in his notebook, and noting their placement, function, and vulnerability to various invaders.

Herman was interested in epidemiology because he read how protozoa, bacteria, and viruses multiplied and spread through a population, especially if there was a poor public health system. A system that lacked a mechanism for identifying and isolating attackers was especially inadequate. He learned about the bubonic plague that ravished Europe, Asia, and Africa during the 14th century, caused by a bacterium that was spread by fleas from small animals. It was estimated to have killed fifty million people. He recalled the Spanish Flu, for which there were rumors that in the United States started in a military training camp. Later it was called the Spanish Flu because Spain was transparent and reported accurately the number of deaths that were occurring there. Reportedly over 675,000 died in the United States out of a population of 100 million. Many medical students, residents, and doctors focused on injuries or diseases that afflicted patients one at a time like they were picking apples off a tree. Herman focused on the whole orchard. *What makes some people more susceptible to communicable diseases? How can we strengthen our immune systems? How can we defend populations once transmission of disease starts between humans?*

Herman used a wide lens in studying medicine, and he was not content to accept what might appear to be inevitable. He used this approach when treating poor Negro patients in Meharry's clinics. A colored woman humming a gospel tune while holding a crying child was one of his first patients. "I see your name is Jessie and is this your boy, Calvin?" Herman began in a comforting manner, while he took the child's temperature and examined his eyes. "What seems to be bothering him?" Herman continued gathering the child's medical history and observing the mother's understanding of good health habits. This knowledge would help Herman formulate instructions for the boy's care. Many of Herman's clinic patients lived not far from the Medical School in the poor sec tions of Nashville. Most were of African descent. They did not have regular evaluations from a family doctor because often they did not have health insurance. Many had crowded unclean living conditions, inadequate diets, and high stress from unemployment or underemployment, as well as crime in their neighborhoods. In examining his patients, it was common to find that they had multiple comorbidities, sometimes aggravated by their environment. Herman wrote extensive progress notes on each patient, recording their complex histories and conditions. Herman's notes were so detailed that a supervising resident claimed that he would never make a living if he spent too much time on a patient's history.

Herman felt *I am putting a band aid on symptoms, the causes of which are lack of primary care and racism that kept these families in unhealthy living conditions. In contrast, some White patients have fewer health problems due to their better nutrition and living arrangements. Generally, if they do have any comorbidities, their conditions are closely monitored because they are more likely to be employed in jobs that offer health insurance.*

✧ ✧ ✧

After the end of Herman's second year, he went home with Margarita and three-year-old Judith to visit his parents. With the car packed they set out for the eight-hour journey through the rolling hills of the Smoky Mountains to Charlotte, North Carolina. Margarita had made sandwiches to eat along the way. If they had stopped at any roadside cafe, they would be directed to sit in a colored section or be denied service. Better to avoid the humiliation or questions from Judith such as "Why?"

When they arrived in Charlotte they drove to the Brooklyn area in the Third Ward, noticing that not much had changed. Houses looked like they could use a coat of paint. Trash was piled up waiting to be hauled away. Old cars with their hoods up dotted front yards waiting for a fix. On-street corners, casting their eyes downward, men gathered to share idle talk. The contrast with the commercial uptown area or the suburbs could not have been starker. They passed a billboard of a crusade by Billy Graham at the First Baptist Church. *Perhaps his message might make White folks notice the inequalities that exist in Charlotte and compel them to do something about it. Maybe they could start with desegregating schools, restaurants, and hospitals. After all, didn't White clergy preach God's love for the least fortunate? How fortunate are descendants of former slaves when they could not go to schools, hospitals, or lunch counters that White people can enjoy?*

Arriving at his parents' house, Herman first saw his dad, Jacob, in the front yard. Before a word was spoken, their eyes met, transmitting pride from the father and gratitude from the son. Walking forward with arms wide open, they embraced, like Herman was a soldier coming home from war. Margarita, holding Judith's hand, entered the house, and was greeted by Betsy shouting, "Oh my God! Judith how you have grown!" Around the kitchen table, as Betsy served apple pie, Herman and Margarita answered questions about living in Nashville and the challenges of the second year at Meharry Medical School.

"Well, just two more years and maybe you will come back here. God knows colored folks here could use a good Negro doctor," Jacob mentioned, hoping to lure Herman and his family back home.

"Maybe you could get an appointment at Good Samaritan Hospital," Betsy offered. Like fishing, the bait was a combination of the father stressing the need and the mother optimistically presenting the possibilities.

Good Samaritan Hospital began during a time of great change in America. After the Civil War people began to understand the value of having hospitals to take care of the sick and injured. The origins of Good Samaritan were rooted in the philosophy of the Episcopal Church to heal, and the determined efforts of Jane Renwick Wilkes. Jane was born in New York City, where she went to school and later married John Wilkes. John graduated first in his class at the Naval Academy. After a distinguished career as a naval officer, he founded the Mecklenburg Flour Mills in 1858 and Iron Works in 1859. Although Jane had nine children, she was very active in affairs with the Saint Peter's Episcopal Church. Along with a group of other White women, Jane raised funds to build Saint Peter's Hospital, North Carolina's first private civilian hospital. Afterward, in keeping with the segregation movement that was gripping the South after the Civil War and reconstruction, Jane set out to establish a hospital for Negro folks. In 1901 Good Samaritan Hospital was built with funds raised by Jane, the Saint Peter's Episcopal Church, and Jane's friends in New York City. Good Samaritan gave Charlotte the distinction of being the only privately funded hospital built exclusively for Negro patients in North Carolina. Then in 1903, the Hospital opened a School of Nursing.

"I do not know, Mom, when I was in high school Good Samaritan Hospital was a facility people did not want to use, because it was a place where people died," Herman commented. Herman again was thinking of his grandfather who died of the 1918 Flu, when Herman was only in the first grade.

"You could change that, Herman. Times are changing," Herman's mother said, "and you could be a part of that change. Besides, I have heard it is still not possible for colored doctors to get on the staff of Saint Peter's or any of the other hospitals that treat White patients."

Betsy's words hung in the air for a long time, like milkweed pods, before Herman, cutting himself another piece of pie, replied, "I must complete medical school, then I want to get some additional training as a resident in internal medicine. In particular, I want to focus on infectious diseases. Then I can treat and help patients like Pappy who may catch a communicable disease. Perhaps I could do that and serve in the military at the same time before coming home." There were nods all around, pleased that Herman had a plan. Like his college football days, he could see the goalposts.

✧   ✧   ✧

Third Year of Medical School

For Herman, the third year of medical school was a relief from the rigors of studying sixteen hours a day and mostly being taught medical facts, theories, and treatments in classrooms with little clinical application. Now the focus was on applying knowledge gleaned through rotations in the few hospitals open to Negro medical students, Hubbard Hospital and Nashville General Hospital.

Herman's challenge during his third year was to establish a balance between his home life and medical school. Margarita was now restarting her career as an elementary school teacher. Judith still attended the daycare facility every weekday. Herman made sure he was studying enough to do well on his national medical exams, going faithfully to his clinical rotations, making progress notes on his hospitalized clinic patients, and being prepared for grand rounds. He started each day by getting up at four in the morning with a pot of coffee and classical music on the radio. Then after two hours of studying, he made breakfast for Margarita and Judith before going to Nashville General for his rotation on the floors. At six-thirty, Herman was dressed in his scrubs, stethoscope draped over his shoulders, seeing patients, and making progress notes. Then at about eight he participated in rounds with an intern, resident, attending physician, and charge nurse, making sure he was prepared to give a brief presentation regarding each patient's condition, any significant clinical changes, and recommendations for treatment. Questions from his colleagues who had the luxury of more experience came fast and forcefully. What was the family history of cardiovascular disease? What did the hemoglobin show? Is the patient hypertensive? Herman went on to do rotations in the emergency room, pediatrics, surgery, and obstetrics, before doing a rotation in outpatient medicine.

Herman was lucky when a Jewish doctor, Dr. Lawrence, opened the first integrated clinic because of his experience treating Negro soldiers during World War II. Dr. Lawrence's compassionate efforts to be a servant leader, treating patients regardless of their skin color, resulted in a boycott of his office by many of his White patients. In addition, Dr. Lawrence experienced alienation from his physician colleagues, as well as threats against his life from unknown racist sources. Herman did a rotation there in outpatient internal medicine and cardiovascular disease. One day after seeing patients all day while receiving guidance from Michael, a second-year resident from Vanderbilt University Hospital, Herman was on his way out. Walking down the corridor past examination rooms, he noticed that Dr. Lawrence was still in his office.

Without thinking Herman turned around and knocked on the door. Since the door was slightly open, he walked in and looked at Dr. Lawrence, who was going over a pile of patient charts. "Can I help you?" Dr. Lawrence said as he lowered his reading glasses, put down his pen, and leaned back in his chair.

At first, Herman was speechless. Standing in front of the founder of this large important clinic, he found it difficult to utter why he was there. "I, I, I wanted to thank you for opening your clinic to colored patients and allowing medical students like myself a chance to come here to rotate and learn. From Hippocrates and all our professors at Meharry, we are taught to be compassionate with our patients. It is refreshing. I am truly grateful to meet someone who embodies compassion by what you started here."

Dr. Lawrence, a big man, balding, with a round face, got up slowly, shook Herman's hand, and sat his large frame on his desk. After a few moments of silence, he said, "I spent years in the military during World War II observing the courageous efforts and injuries of Black soldiers. They were often segregated and treated unfairly. I thought if the Lord was kind enough to let me come home to my wife and children, there would be no more separation of people in my life. All would be treated as children of God."

✧ ✧ ✧

Fourth Year Medical School

Herman's fourth year started with an academic challenge, preparing for, and passing the national Clinical Skills and Assessment Exam, given to all soon-to-be graduating medical school students to measure their competency to move on to become doctors.

Herman finished more rotations, concentrating on his interest in infectious disease. Dr. Wrigley, who was Director of Infectious Disease at Nashville General Hospital informed Herman that the United States' public health programs have improved drinking water and sanitation, as well as had great successes with vaccinations. As a result, there had been a decline in communicable diseases since 1920. Herman asked Dr. Wrigley, "Have prevention and control measures changed at all recently?"

"Unfortunately," Dr. Wrigley said, "now the low incidence of infectious disease has made the public less motivated to pay for and participate in control programs, resulting in negative consequences for the whole community."

"Really, given the high cost of a pandemic you would think it would be a good investment to pay for preventive measures," Herman replied, thinking of the cost of the 1918 pandemic, which took 675,000 lives and shredded the economy.

Dr. Wrigley commented, "Parents who question the risk-benefit of vaccines may refuse to immunize their children, which leads to a greater probability of epidemics. We must be cheerleaders, championing the results of good practices and cautioning against behavior that could have disastrous consequences. Not investing in vaccine research, good public health, or having access to primary healthcare can be a very dangerous course to follow. For example, the smallpox vaccine was introduced in the United States around 1800 by Dr. Ben Waterhouse, allowing us to almost eliminate this dreadful disease by 1927. But when vaccination rates decreased, the annual incidence of a less severe virus of smallpox continued until the disease was recently finally eradicated."

During his rotation Herman stayed long hours in the Infectious Disease Department talking to Dr. Wrigley, reading journals, and following patients who had communicable diseases. Some of these patients became infected during trips abroad. Some from the transmission from domesticated farm animals and some from animals in the smoky mountains of Tennessee. A few of the diseases Herman treated included: meningitis, pneumonia, tuberculosis, influenza, brucellosis, typhoid fever, encephalitis, and rabies.

✦ ✦ ✦

Post Graduate Training and Uncle Sam

In the middle of Herman's fourth year, he began thinking more about post-graduate training while serving in the armed forces. Following his internship and residency, he would be required to spend two years in active service as a Captain in the Army. Another option would be to stay in the Army and complete a fellowship in infectious disease after his residency. Then fulfill the remainder of his service obligation in the United States Army Reserves. Given Herman's interest in starting a private practice, the latter option seemed more likely. After careful consideration, he was drawn to Walter Reed General Hospital like a moth to a flame. The Hospital was named after Major Walter Reed, an Army epidemiologist physician, who led a team that discovered that yellow fever was transmitted by mosquitoes, rather than by direct human contact.

Herman discussed going to Walter Reed with Margarita. "The largest biomedical research facility of the United States Department of Defense is housed at Walter Reed Army Institute of Research," Herman said enthusiastically. "I read where it traces its origins back before the turn of the century and claims to be the first school of public health and preventive medicine in the world."

"Would we live there in Washington, D.C.?" Margarita asked.

"Yes, I believe we would live in subsidized military housing on the campus.

Judith would go to school nearby," Herman added.

It would be a giant opportunity to live in Washington D.C. and be in the Army to serve our country. The possibilities are endless. If only I could get accepted, Herman thought. Prejudice and segregation were still much alive in the Army. Two leaders of African American descent were about to change things. Asa Philip Randolph had organized the Brotherhood of Sleeping Car Porters in 1925. Grant Reynolds was a black chaplain (having served stateside during World War II), who was an attorney and politically active civil rights leader. Together Randolph and Reynolds in October 1947 organized the Committee Against Jim Crow in Military Service and Training. President Roosevelt was compelled to prohibit discrimination in the defense industry, but Jim Crow practices and prejudices still held back most people of color. Herman had recently learned from his classmate George that Randolph and Reynolds were organizing to change things for the better for blacks in the military by encouraging Negroes to boycott the draft. George said it's possible President Truman will issue an executive order soon establishing a policy of equality of treatment and opportunity for all US military persons regardless of race, color, or religion.

Finally, a few days before his training at Meharry Medical School ended, Herman received a letter indicating his acceptance to the Internal Medicine Residency Program at Walter Reed General Hospital. Herman was excited to continue his journey of learning as much as he could about medicine. His goals remained to prevent as much as possible infectious illnesses that had the potential of affecting large numbers of people.

For graduation Herman's parents, Jacob and Betsy drove from Charlotte through the Smoky Mountains to Nashville and the campus of Meharry Medical School. Before everyone was seated,

Herman introduced George. Jacob's interest in history was stirred when he learned that George served with the Blank Panthers, the famous World War II African American tank battalion. Jacob shook George's hand, locked eyes with him, and said, "Right on, George! The Black Panthers made our people proud, scaring the heebie-jeebies out of those German boys, who were intoxicated, believing their race was superior to the rest of us."

Herman sat with his classmates in white folding chairs. Meharry medical students that day were privileged to receive the sage words of Dr. Louis Wright, a physician of color whose father, Ceah Ketchan Wright, was born a slave, but amazingly after emancipation went on to become a doctor, finishing medical school as valedictorian of his class. Dr. Louis Wright graduated from Harvard Medical School. Dr. Louis Wright joined the Army Medical Corps, serving as a lieutenant during World War I. While stationed in France he introduced intradermal vaccination for smallpox. (The earliest historical evidence of mankind suffering from smallpox, Herman had learned, dated to the 3rd century BC in Egyptian mummies. He also knew that the disease historically occurred in bursts.) Dr. Louis Wright in the war to end all wars was awarded the Purple Heart after exposure to German poison gas warfare. Dr. Louis Wright was the first Negro physician to serve with distinction as a surgeon at Harlem Hospital. Many of his initiatives for improving quality were later followed by hospitals throughout the United States. After acknowledging the support of parents and professors, Dr. Wright called upon the students to be leaders, committing themselves not only to serve their communities but also to advance medical knowledge that benefits all of mankind.

In a strong voice, Dr. Wright said,

> "There is a great need for doctors, particularly in African American communities, to treat diseases that are causing our people to suffer unnecessarily and shortening their lives. Some of you will go on to academia, training tomorrow's physicians or engaging in clinical

research, spawning breakthroughs that disproportionately affect populations of color like sickle cell anemia. Others of you will answer the call to compassionately treat patients. In doing so, keep one eye focused on the matter at hand, like a patient's bleeding or having an unknown fever. But with your other eye observe what is happening to groups of patients. That is where your steely resolve, nurtured here at Meharry, will have its most impact."

Chapter Thirteen

RESIDENCY IN INTERNAL MEDICINE

FOLLOWING GRADUATION HERMAN, Margarita and Judith moved to Washington, D.C. to start Herman's residency in Internal Medicine. They arranged to live in a house near Walter Reed General Hospital. As part of his entrance into the Army Herman had to leave his family and do an accelerated officer's training at the US Army Medical Department and School at Fort Sam Houston in San Antonio, Texas.

As he left the plane at the San Antonio Airport Herman and other officers were greeted by Lieutenant Jonathan Hickey, who drove them to Fort Sam Houston. Herman checked into the officer's barracks. Orientation consisted of being introduced to the Army's traditions, completing the Army Basic Officer Leadership Course, and performing medical procedures under the supervision of a more senior physician. Through his friend, George, Herman had learned about the heroic exploits of World War II black soldiers who earned praise from General Patton. Yet when

Herman entered the officer's mess hall for dinner the segregation, he viewed there hit him like a punch in his gut.

Herman enjoyed working at the hospital doing medical procedures. Fort Sam Houston Hospital was a center for patients undergoing treatment for burns suffered during the war. Often their treatment lasted for months. With nothing to do in between treatments, these soldiers were idle, telling war stories, playing cards, or drinking, and wasting away in their barracks. Herman visited the lab of the Infection Disease Department and spoke to the physicians on staff. He was impressed by their professionalism and commitment to the Army's Medical Corps. In meeting Dr. Nicholson, Director of Infectious Disease, Herman asked, "What kind of diseases do you see here?"

Dr. Nicholson responded, "We have patients sent to us from bases all over the world. During the first World War, the United States lost almost as many troops to the 1918 Spanish Flu pandemic as it did in battles themselves. That is why it is so important to do research to identify pathogens and take preventive measures to keep them from spreading amongst our troops. We also must guard against biological warfare, where an enemy might attack us using a deadly infectious virus or bacteria against our soldiers or civilian population."

"How do we prepare and stop such an attack?" Herman inquired.

"Not easy. You must be able to identify the biological agent quickly and develop an antidote or antibiotic, or administer a vaccine beforehand as a precaution," Dr. Nicholson commented.

Herman began to contemplate the possibilities. *Enemies secretly introducing communicable diseases into the water supply in major US cities; terrorists inserting a bug into the air handling systems of skyscrapers, or adversaries infecting livestock with a communicable disease parasite. Detecting such events and determining who is responsible would be difficult. The possibility that a germ produced by a county could contaminate and sicken the people in the environment where the organism was created, or the potential of an attack on an adversary spreading beyond the intended border creating a global pandemic were plausible. These perhaps unpre-*

ventable adverse consequences of germ warfare provided extreme importance to the field of epidemiology, infectious disease, and the need for disease prevention and risk management.

✧   ✧   ✧

On Sunday, taking a break from studying and working, Herman was walking back from church, when he came across a large grassy field with bleachers on one side. Upon inquiring he found out this was the area where soldiers paraded for various ceremonies like graduation. It was a warm Texas day. The sun was breaking through the clouds. A lonely flag near a reviewing stand was as still as the black crow that watched from atop the flagpole. Herman noticed a group of soldiers in shorts playing touch football. As he looked, a soldier yelled for him to join them as they were short one player. Herman gladly agreed and went home to change clothes. Running back to the field, he was first assigned a position as a defensive end. After a few running plays, the opposing quarterback threw a pass to a wide receiver running in Herman's direction. Herman ran fast, jumped high in the air, and snagged the football. Herman showed why at Johnson Smith University they called him the Rocket. He faked left, then darted right towards the side of the field, then ran back to the left as he made his way up the other sideline. Eventually, he scored a touchdown. As his teammates high-fived and patted him on the back, Herman felt grateful for that small moment of acceptance justly deserved.

✧   ✧   ✧

Remembering the Alamo

Herman enjoyed experiencing San Antonio, which was at the crossroads of many ethnic cultures. Its diversity could be seen in the city's art, music, festivals, architecture, and cuisine. Herman liked sampling the spicy food among the many restaurants built a few years earlier along the serpentine San Antonio River. The renovation of the meandering river showed what could be done to revitalize an unattractive narrow stream into a tourist attraction. People of different ethnicities had worked together to give the city a lively nightlife and cultural focal point. Like any visitor, Herman had to see the sites and learn the long history of the city of San Antonio and its historical Alamo.

Initially, in 1718 San Antonio de Valero, later referred to as the Alamo served as a mission. It was built in the 18th century by Roman Catholic missionaries to educate the local American Indians and convert them to Christianity. Several military units occupied the Alamo over time. The first was a Spanish garrison. Then Mexican soldiers, following the Mexican War of Independence from Spain, occupied the facility. Some say that the complex got its name Alamo because it is the Spanish word for cottonwood trees that were growing nearby. Others say the name came from Mexican soldiers, who in 1920 may have referred to it in honor of Alamo de Parras, the hometown of some of the soldiers. The Alamo played a vital role in the Texas Revolution against Mexico. Like any visitor, Herman had to see a place that had such a rich history for Texans.

Anglo Americans began settling in the northern area of Mexico, now called Texas. Some of these families wanted to farm cotton and use slave labor. In 1829, however, the Guerrero Decree abolished slavery throughout Mexico. It was a decision that increased tensions between some of the Anglo-American slave-owning settlers and the Mexican government. As more and more Anglo Americans migrated to northern Mexico, eventually it led to the Texan Revolution. The Republic of Texas was formed in 1836. During the revolution, Mexican forces surrendered the Alamo, which was then reoccupied by a small force of Texan patriots. Afterward, a Mexican force of thousands, led by General Antonio Lopez de Santa Anna, began a siege of the fort. Though vastly outnumbered, the Alamo's two hundred defenders, commanded by James Bowie, William Travis, and the famed frontiersman Davy Crockett, held out for thirteen days before the

Mexican forces finally overpowered them in what became known as The Battle of the Alamo. For Texans, The Battle of the Alamo became a symbol of their struggle for independence, which they won in 1835. Statehood was granted in 1845. Eclipsed by the story of the Alamo was the role that slavery played in encouraging some Anglo Americans to fight their Mexican neighbors so these same Anglo-American settlers could continue the practice of slavery.

✧ ✧ ✧

Walter Reed Army Medical Center

Herman completed his basic officer's training at Fort Sam Houston, and he witnessed the opening of the Brooks Army Medical Center, the Army's finest academic hospital and trauma center. He then returned to Walter Reed Army Medical Center. After spending a leisurely tour of the area with family, he prepared to start his internship or first-year residency on Monday. Margarita wished him well as she dropped Herman off on his first day. Herman was wearing the short white jacket that all first-year residents wore. However, anxiety was building inside him. *During medical school, I learned about function and theory, now I am going to be responsible for patients on my own. I wonder if I have it in me to handle my nervousness and the intensity of this job.*

Arriving at the Department of Medicine office, Herman was greeted by Ms. Stanley, Office Manager, to register and receive his schedule for the year. Herman shook hands with his fellow residents, some of whom had graduated from George Washington University Medical School, John Hopkins, University of Pennsylvania, Yale University, and Thomas Jefferson University. Herman considered himself lucky, as he was the only intern of color. Herman's duties involved taking care of patients, writing follow-up orders, answering nurses' questions, and supervising medical students. His assignment initially included the general medical floor on Three South and the Emergency Room.

As he made his way to Three South Herman took the stairs to avoid people, climbing them two at a time. Sweat was pouring off him as if his body knew something he did not. Herman thought about his fellow interns. They were from prestigious medical schools, had postures erect like a 2 by 4, and showed confidence seeping from them like blood oozing out of a raw wound. He was perplexed. So much was riding on him being able to get through this part of his training. As he walked down the corridor on the third floor, his nerves were on edge. He felt the glare of the white fluorescent lights, inhaled the smell of alcohol, and supposed that people everywhere were staring at him.

He ducked into a men's room. Washing his hands, Herman looked into the mirror and saw emptiness. *People are counting on me, yet I am ridged, fearful of letting Margarita, Judith, and my parents down. Why is this happening?*

A hand rested upon his shoulder from a tall man who had just entered the men's room and was now standing behind him. It belonged to a doctor with pale skin, light hair, and blue eyes, wearing a gleaming full-length white physician's lab coat. Clearing his throat, the doctor said in a deep, strong voice, "At some time we all went through what you're experiencing. You will overcome it. I know, because I struggled, had doubts, and considered quitting, but got through it. You will learn, not only from nurses, physicians, and technicians but also from your patients. The wisdom you receive will be like a stream you will drink from the whole remainder of your life. Diversity of patients, even those having the same disease will enlighten you." Herman turned to face this voice that cut through the silence of the restroom. "Being a doctor is a privilege and an opportunity to learn. As we gain knowledge, our confidence grows, and we give back. To do our job well we need people from different backgrounds, and cultures, who see things others do not see."

Herman thanked the doctor. Looking back at the mirror Herman could see some of his former self appearing through the fog in the mirror. Taking a big breath, he felt better. He left the restroom walking slowly and then more rapidly down the corridor. Herman saw the physician who had previously spoken to him waiting for an elevator. Herman asked a nurse nearby, "Excuse me, can you tell me the name of that physician?"

With a smile on her face, the nurse responded, "That is our Chief of Surgery, Dr. John Armstrong. He is the leading cardiothoracic surgeon in the country."

✧ ✧ ✧

The Perils of Internship

Taking a break for lunch Herman went to the cafeteria. He put a sandwich and an apple on his tray and sat down in the doctor's area, pleased to see many of his fellow interns there. Tim O'Reilly was from Virginia. Tim was later nicknamed Bones. Tim's father, an orthopedic surgeon, wanted Tim to follow in his footsteps. Eagle Breckenridge from Bethesda, Maryland, whose family owned a publishing business, was fondly named Hawkeye by Herman. Winston Goodman was a good-looking intern from Baltimore. Winston's father was a cardiologist, and Winston was given the name Heartbreaker by one of the nurses. Allen Jenson from Silver Springs, Maryland, whose father was a pediatrician and mother a psychologist, shortened his handle to AJ. Josh Arnold from Atlanta was called JoJo. Herman's moniker was Foot, given to him by one of the colored orderlies, who knew Herman had played football. All were eating fast as if they only had a moment before returning to the front lines of battle.

"I finally got to insert an arterial line successfully," Heartbreaker proudly stated.

"Was that red-haired nurse, Mary Jo holding your hand?" AJ jabbed kiddingly.

"The ER looked like a war zone this morning. Accident on the freeway. Ambulances brought us four injuries. One with an arm hanging like a shirt on a clothesline. Blood all over the gurneys. There was no time to think. Thank God for the nurses' barking orders." Hawkeye said, still pumped up.

Bones, not wanting to be left out, chimed in, "I just wish I could do something right the first time."

Then everyone erupted in laughter as JoJo asked, "Does anyone know where I can go to have a nervous breakdown?"

Like players breaking from a football huddle, they all stood up, wished each other well, and scurried to absorb knowledge and gain confidence. The insecurity of not knowing slowly began the long process of drifting away, like smoke from a chimney.

✧   ✧   ✧

After an insane day with no time to spare, Herman rounded on his last patient. He did his hand off, relating what was happening with his patients to JoJo, who looked thoroughly drained and washed up.

"Now JoJo do not go to sleep on Mr. Webber. He is in AFib. I gave him some heparin. He is having some flashbacks from his service in the Army during the war. He landed in Sicily and saw a lot of action," Herman related.

"Right now, I could use a good crap to get rid of all this anxiety, or maybe a sedative the size of a pillow. You know, like the one named after Saint Barbara," JoJo said, referring to a barbiturate drug, barbital. "Barbital," he added "was named after a beautiful maiden, who in the third century became a saint after her father beheaded her for converting to Christianity."

"I know. I am coming back to be on call. Hopefully, I will get some sleep in the on-call room. There is no one to consult at night. I'll be on my own. Like being on a leaky boat in the middle of the ocean with no life preserver waiting for a hurricane," Herman replied, as he headed for the stairs to leave.

Outside Herman took a bus home for a quick dinner with Margarita and Judith, before coming back. When he entered the door, he was greeted. "Well, you look totally worn out. How did it go?" Margarita said as she tossed a salad and inspected the pasta boiling.

"It is very hectic. Everyone is asking you questions, and answers are sometimes hard to come by. One must consider all the variances of a disease, what comorbidities are also present, and what the hell occurred that brought the patient to the hospital. It is like the world is in the room when you see a patient," Herman lamented. "You see the concern on the faces of patients. There was often panic in the eyes of other interns that were leaving the shift. Then when you learn the patient's history, you feel you are not the only person facing innumerable challenges. You realize what's happening outside. Families are struggling to feed their children. Men are having nightmares about the war. Women are abused in dead marriages. Everyone is looking at you for good health answers. Some of the patients are beyond hope, near Death's door waiting for him to come in. The attendings want you to do everything to keep them alive, work them up for comorbidities that will never change the timetable of their death. Interns send these patients for extensive GI XRays, inserting tube feedings, or putting them on respirators."

"Why all the intervention, which sounds like it would discomfort these patients if they were terminal?" Margareta asked, looking perplexed.

"Some say it is Moola."

"What?"

"The private docs charge the patient for each day they are in the hospital. The laboratory gets more money for each test. The radiologist gets paid for each radiology exam. The hospital charges for each day a patient is in there. Everyone has their hand on the patient's wallet, except for the interns, who must follow up on each test done and watch their patients suffer.

"Let me shower."

"What's for dinner? It smells good," Herman said with a forced smile and a needed hug.

✧ ✧ ✧

Herman drove himself back to the hospital to be on call, feeling like he never left the place. He found JoJo in the coffee room looking worse than when Herman left him. As they began their handoff, JoJo commented, "Mr. Thompson, the guy with the broken teeth, was having some post-traumatic stress with chest pain, so I started an arterial line, gave him oxygen, nitro, and a barbiturate. Took one myself. It is great for the nerves."

"JoJo, you took a barbiturate. I thought you were just kidding before about doing it. That's crazy!"

"Well, it helped me cope with all the doubts and angst that were overloading my brain. Made me drowsy, so on this shift, I drank about a gallon of coffee."

Jojo and Herman went through reviewing the patients, noting any changes in their condition, what had been done for them, and reviewed any pending orders. Both Jojo and Herman felt vulnerable because of their limited experience and knowledge in handling medical treatments. Plus, both knew many of, but possibly not all, the multiple comorbidities of the patients. These factors made them wonder if some of the treatments that had been given were going to make the patients' conditions even worse. They hoped not. They agreed that they were sort of like hunters trying to shoot a charging quarry with a shotgun, good perhaps at short range if well-aimed, but scattered, messy, and less deadly at a distance.

"What about Mr. Clayborn, the Black overweight man with the balding gray hair in Room 306, who I admitted this afternoon?" Herman asked.

"I do not know much. He may have diabetic ketoacidosis. He was vomiting with abdominal pain, weakness, and seemed confused, but that may be his usual state," JoJo said half-jokingly.

"I doubt it. Did you notice anything unusual about his history? Did you see the hat he was wearing?" Herman asked.

"No."

"The insignia on his hat is from the 761 Battalion, a tank unit called the Black Panthers. This guy saw some bad stuff when deployed. Colored people have a higher incidence of diabetes. Being in a tank with little physical activity, eating an excessive amount of candy bars, and gaining weight may have together led to his diabetic condition. I will continue to replace his fluids, electrolytes and provide insulin therapy as needed. Probably consult an endocrinologist as well. Thanks, JoJo, you did a good job. Now go home. Have a beer for breakfast to offset the caffeine, and pass out," Herman ordered.

"Beer and a shot of bourbon! After a year of this you will not find me in the doctor's lounge. My toes will be tagged, and I will be in the morgue."

Herman mused. *It is amazing how much baggage patients have, and how important it is to do their history thoroughly. So many things contributed to a patient's condition. Knowing the patients well is key to understanding the origins of their diseases, what drugs they can tolerate, or how best to motivate them to change their behavior. Some doctors are better than others at learning the subtle aspects of a patient's history. Sometimes blindness or lack of empathy is due to cultural differences or not having similar experiences.*

Herman thought again of the diabetic patient, Mr. Clayborn. Herman reflected. *Would a White intern growing up in an upscale neighborhood take the time to understand why his blood sugar was high? Diversity,* he thought, *having dissimilar backgrounds, race, or orientations, is as important in medicine as they are in art and music.*

Herman then settled in with a new admission, Mr. McDonald, a 37-year-old, red-haired Navy man with a big tattoo of a serpent on his arm, who had a fever of unknown origin. Herman started an IV on him while doing his history and a physical. Herman asked, "Did you see any action during the War? I see you were in the Navy.

"Action! Did I see action? Buddy, I was on Mighty Mo, the biggest, worst battleship ever built. When our nine 16-inch guns blew, it rattled Okinawa 24 miles away. Last September, when the Japs surrendered on our deck, General MacArthur gave a short speech. Called for a new day of tolerance, justice, freedom, and peace, as 255 allied ships assembled in Tokyo Harbor and 1000 planes flew overhead," Mr. McDonald said, bursting with pride to have been a part of the US Missouri Battleship crew.

"Wow hats off to Might Mo! Did you do any R and R off the ship, Herman asked, thinking perhaps the sailor might have caught some infection in the Pacific.

"Yes, we went ashore in Manila after the war was over."

Herman, scratching his head and thinking he might be onto something, ordered a blood culture.

Chapter Fourteen

SECOND YEAR RESIDENCY

ERMAN WAS HAPPY to complete his internship and start his second year of residency. He would be supervising interns and medical students as well as acting as the principal resource for the attending physicians. Additionally, at Walter Reed, he oversaw the medical clinic, where patients were seen following their discharge from the Hospital. Although the pace was hectic, Herman now had more time to teach, read, and gain confidence as a physician. Remembering what he went through as an intern made Herman less demanding of his subordinates. As busy as they were, he instructed the interns to stay calm, develop a good bedside manner to allay the patients' fears, and thereby help to ensure the patients' trust in them as new doctors. His interns followed this advice, all but one of them, Randy Pearson, who needed more work.

Randy, called Dork by his fellow interns, came from a wealthy family. His father at the age of fifty-five had sold the oil business he had inherited from his dad. Out of boredom, Dork's father decided to become a congressman. Randy went to Avon Old Farms, a boarding school in Connecticut. For his undergraduate degree in Biology

Randy attended Yale. With some pull from his dad, Randy received his M.D. degree from George Washington University.

Randy sometimes lacked focus. He was easily distracted from his intern duties when talking to a medical student or to a pretty nurse. One day he admitted Mr. Carmine, who was struggling with the flu and atrial fibrillation. Mr. Carmine was having some difficulty breathing. Randy, in a rush to take Mr. Carmine's history, overlooked that Mr. Carmine took aspirin several times that day for a headache. To treat Mr. Carmine's atrial fibrillation, Randy gave him heparin, a blood thinner. Mr. Carmine had served in the Army and saw action in North Africa during the Second World War. He had a large family. A few buddies from his Army unit and his wife were with him at his bedside when Mr. Carmine became very dizzy, started vomiting, and developed a much stronger headache than ever before. An iatrogenic adverse medical event, that is, a medical event caused by the treatment rendered by a doctor to a patient, had just happened.

Mr. Carmine's blood, already thinned by the aspirin, was further thinned by the heparin. Possibly, as a result, Mr. Carmin suffered a cerebellar hemorrhagic stroke. Mrs. Carmine was in disbelief when she witnessed her husband's condition worsening. Randy, realizing that Mr. Carmine was probably having a stroke, tried to console the Carmine family, but he was perceived as lacking sincerity and empathy. Because of this, they did not trust him. Randy ran to call Herman at home about what was happening.

Upon hearing the details from Dork, Herman stopped eating his dinner and rushed to Mr. Carmine's bedside. Herman immediately took control of Mr. Carmine's medical care. He reversed the anticoagulation caused by the heparin, performed the necessary emergency procedure, ordered the appropriate studies and medications, and requested a neurosurgery consultation. The neurosurgeon determined surgery was indicated to treat the bleeding in Mr. Carmine's brain. Herman felt a deep responsibility for the actions of his interns. He was upset at Mr. Carmine's condition and Randy's shortcomings in communicating with the family. Sensing the family's concern, Herman, in a calm manner, explained that sometimes in managing one condition, there is a risk that a patient may not tolerate the treatment prescribed as well as would other patients.

"Mrs. Carmine, I can assure you Walter Reed Hospital has the best specialists in the United States. That is why Senators, Presidents, and people from all over the world come here to be treated." Herman's words were full of confidence, conviction, and support for the Hospital and its staff. Herman realized that trust was the foundation of healthcare. For the benefit of Mr. Carmine, he needed to restore the family's faith in the treatment plan.

(Following a surgical procedure to reduce pressure on his brain, Mr. Carmine began to stabilize, although he was confused, and his coordination and speech were erratic. His prognosis was better because of the surgery and correct treatment, but Mr. Carmine would eventually need months of physical therapy as well as speech and occupational therapy following his discharge to a nursing home.)

Herman found Randy in the doctor's lounge sipping coffee. Herman poured himself a cup and waited until Randy and he were alone. "Randy, in reading over your medical history of Mr. Carmine, is there anything you feel might be missing?" Herman began.

"I did not know until his wife mentioned it later, that he took aspirin over the last few days for a headache, " Randy responded. "I asked Mr. Carmine if he was taking any prescription drugs, but in hindsight, I should have also asked him if he was taking any over-the-counter medications. If Mr. Carmine had informed me, he was taking aspirin, I may not have ordered heparin for his atrial fibrillation, at least not until I was able to discuss the drug combination with a hospital pharmacist, the patient, and his family." Randy concluded.

"Randy, this has been a learning experience for both of us. I have found that taking and accurately recording the patient's history gives all doctors involved as clear a picture of the patient's medical situation as possible. Medical history is indispensable in formulating a roadmap on how best to treat those under our care. Taking a thorough history builds a positive relationship and trust.

The confidence patients have in their physicians and nurses leads to better acceptance of our plans for treating them. Randy, no one questions your intelligence or your medical knowledge, but you must learn to completely devote yourself to your patient's care and well-being. Moreover, the better things we can honestly say about our hospital and colleagues, the more we can avoid malpractice litigation if something does go wrong," Herman calmly mentioned.

"Randy you are from Texas, I know you have a big heart and care about others. This is just one learning opportunity among many you and I will experience throughout our careers. Stay close to Mr. Carmine. I am going home to finish my dinner. Call me if I can help," Herman, putting his hand on Randy's shoulder, said as he rose to leave.

✧ ✧ ✧

The Sites of Washington Junior Year

As a junior-year resident, Herman had more free time, so when he was not at the Hospital on weekends, he and his family took in the sites that Washington D.C. had to offer. First up was a trip to the Washington Monument. Margareta packed a picnic lunch. Judith was all excited. She had learned about the monument at school.

"It was started before the Civil War and was completed many years after it ended," Judith said like a National Park Ranger.

"That is right Judith. Some of your ancestors helped build it, cutting stone from quarries in Maryland, and working at the construction site. Our people were involved. Slaves also built George Washington's home in Mount Vernon," Margarita added to the history lesson.

Herman and his family began the long climb up the winding Washington Monument staircase to the eye of the obelisk. From there they could see the White House, Capitol, and the Potomac River. Coming back down, they spread out a blanket on the ground nearby and had a picnic.

"There is a great deal of history here, and people of color were a big part of it," Margarita began with the voice of a teacher who knew the contribution enslaved African Americans made to the development of Washington D.C. "Many leaders of our nation owned slaves. George Washington, for instance, became a slave owner at the age of eleven. At his death, at age 67 he had at his Mount Vernon estate a total of 317 enslaved people that he managed as property. Of these, George Washington owned 124, and Martha Washington, his wife had 153. Knowing it was wrong, George Washington in his will called for the emancipation of the slaves he outright owned after the eventual death of Martha. Not wanting to wait, Martha carried out her husband's wishes a year after George's death. Martha Washington, I read, could never free a single enslaved person she owned from her first husband before her death. Her slaves after her death became the property of her grandchildren," Margarita concluded.

Herman sat and listened to the voices of Margarita and Judith. *So spiritual, as if they were singing a hymn of history in the church.* He thought of his own knowledge of US history from his days teaching it in the Third Ward High School. He contemplated the lives of enslaved persons building the White House and the Capital.

His thoughts drifted, like a cloud-changing shape overhead. *He once again pictured his grandparents and their struggles at the White Oak Plantation and becoming free once they arrived in Canada. Visions and sounds of a whip cracking, as his grandfather felt the lash, were imagined almost simultaneously with images of slaves constructing edifices dedicated to equality and freedom. Multiple emotions filled his mind until his thoughts were interrupted.*

"Herman, it is time to go," Margarita said, shaking Herman from his reflections.

✧   ✧   ✧

Being Inspired by The Lincoln Memorial

Another Sunday after Church the family set out to visit the Lincoln Memorial. Herman knew the history of the Memorial as well as he knew that of the Washington Monument. With bursting pride, as he and his family climbed the steps of the monument, he looked up at Lincoln's twenty-seven-foot-tall statue. Herman thought of the stress Lincoln must have experienced as President. *Lincoln guided a divided nation through a war to right a wrong begun many years before when slavery was introduced to the thirteen colonies by British and Dutch merchants.*

This Memorial is also a symbol of the good that comes with perseverance. Herman recalled that Eleanor Roosevelt, an honorary member of the Daughters of the American Revolution, resigned her membership in protest when this all-White heritage association refused to permit Marian Andersen (a prominent singer known in both the United States and Europe) to have a concert at Constitution Hall in 1939 because she was Black. When the concert, with Eleanor and President Roosevelt's help, was finally moved to the Lincoln Memorial, an integrated crowd of 75,000 people showed up. Music filled their ears as the hope of freedom filled their minds. (Marian

134

was to sing again 24 years later at the Lincoln Memorial when an African American Baptist minister named Martin Luther King, Jr. asked her to perform prior to his sharing with the audience of over 250,000 persons **his "Dream" for the country he loved.)**

Chapter Fifteen

THIRD YEAR RESIDENT

I T WAS A hot day in July when Herman started the final year
of his residency in internal medicine. He had gained knowledge, grown more confident, and appreciated the opportunity
to be practicing at the finest medical center for the United States
military and government staff. He began the year with an assessment of where he thought the gaps were in his learning to be an
independent practicing physician. His goals for the year included
learning more about endocrinology and immunology, as well as
identifying doctors with credentials and renowned reputations
like Jake Spencer M.D. who could write letters on his behalf for a
fellowship in infectious disease. Herman knew he had to keep up
his studies to take the internal medicine boards and licensing exam
in North Carolina if he hoped to practice thereafter for his fellowship. Herman found that in his senior year, he was called upon to
supervise and give consultation more than in his previous years.
He liked the fact that junior residents felt comfortable asking him
to examine their patients or asking him for comments after grand
rounds. Herman thought it was his calling to go beyond just car-

ing for patients. He wanted to be a leader, a teacher, valued for his specialized knowledge and for principles that would help his people reach equality and civil justice.

As a third-year resident, Herman rotated to many of the subspecialties of medicine. First was endocrinology, with Doctor Comstock, a blond, blue-eyed physician from Connecticut with a purple birthmark on his neck shaped like the State of West Virginia. Herman was fascinated by how complex endocrinologically the human body was, and how conditions like diabetes mellitus or thyroid dysfunctions could affect other parts of the body. He noted that diabetes affected many patients of color. People with thyroid disorders often had low energy, sometimes comorbidly, many were overweight, had hypertension, and/or heart problems. Herman next rotated to hematology with Doctor Brodie, one of the few physicians at Walter Reed Hospital of African descent. Dr. Brodie, like Herman, played football in college and liked jazz music. Herman knew from his medical training thus far a lot about the different circulating blood cells, the blood vessels and plasma composition, and the bone marrow involved with the hematologic diseases, but working with Doctor Brodie gave him a different perspective. Before Herman thought he was on an airplane looking down, now he was at ground level seeing the details of blood disorders like leukemia and bone marrow diseases. A condition that especially interested Herman was sickle cell anemia, which almost exclusively affected those of African descent. The reason for this was hypothesized to be natural selection. In the tropical areas of Africa, malaria, which was carried from person to person by mosquitoes, was an endemic killer of many in the population for centuries. The bodies of people in this region by natural selection evolved DNA mutations that protected them from getting malaria. One of these mutations that were passed down from generation to generation and were able to prevent malaria in Africans was a mutation that also caused the person to have sickle cell trait or disease.

Over lunch after seeing a patient who had sickle cell anemia, Doctor Brodie commented, "You and I probably will not ever get malaria, living where we do in the United States. We could be carriers of the sickle cell mutation. When a man and a woman who carry the gene for sickle cell trait have a child, there is a one in four chance of the child being born with sickle cell disease."

Herman responded, "Can we test for the trait to counsel couples contemplating having children?"

"Not yet. I and others are working on research that hopefully in time will improve our treatment of this disease. I think it is a gene mutation that instructs the development of red blood cells. It is only a hypothesis, but I am interested in finding the answer, as it is important for our people," Doctor Brodie added.

Herman commented, "I can also think of needed breakthroughs in research identifying mechanisms of resistance to communicable diseases. I can imagine someday it might be possible to speed up our beneficial natural selection mutation process of altering genes, making individuals immune to certain infectious diseases, not through vaccinations, but through modifying genes."

"Reasons for optimism, Herman," Doctor Brody responded as he got up from lunch.

The next rotation was cardiology with Doctor Kelly, a big Irishman with dark hair and greenish eyes. When walking Doctor Kelly looked like a slightly bent-over fullback like he was counting his steps. Doctor Kelly had a positive attitude, a great sense of humor, and compassion for his patients that set him apart from other physicians. He often met with a family while sitting on a chair next to a patient's bed, smiling, reassuring both patient and family that what he recommended would make the patient better. His warm feeling towards others was apparent to all who knew him. Herman learned as much from Doctor Kelly about the humane way to treat patients as he did about cardiology.

Over a cup of coffee in the nurse's station, Doctor Kelly told Herman, "Let your whole body assess what is going on with each patient. Let your mind be on the bed with them. It is not enough to ask them how they feel. You must feel it too. You will know if they are afraid. Let your patients know you understand. Build their trust that you and the staff will help them get better. Hold their hand. Let them know what you are going to do, and that you are in this together. Connect with them. You will then do a better job figuring out what is wrong with them and get their help to assist you in their treatment. One more thing, Herman, when you leave a patient's room, you and the patient should both feel better."

Doctor Kelly, as gentle and caring as he could be, was not shy about making a direct point with his patients. Herman observed one patient, Armando, during rounds with Doctor Kelly. Armando appeared to be in a hurry to get out of the hospital after he had recovered from a brief blackout spell. Armando worked hard to support his large family. He was not aware of how lucky he was that the milk truck he was driving was not going very fast when he became unconscious. After the accident, Armando was brought by ambulance to the hospital. Doctor Kelly, being on call to take any cardiac patient admitted from the Emergency Room, was assigned to care for Armando. Dr. Kelly sat on the bed next to Armando's wife, Maria. After a series of tests, Dr. Kelly determined he may have passed out due to an irregular heartbeat or arrhythmia. Doctor Kelly prescribed some medication and instructed Armando to come to his office after his discharge in a week for follow-up. Dr. Kelly was a strong advocate of changing behavior to improve one's health. He had read recent studies about the harmful effects of smoking. Dr. Kelly could sense the relief in Maria's face, acknowledging that she knew Armando was lucky this time.

"Armando, do you love your wife? Do you love your children? I hear you have seven. That is quite an accomplishment!"

Armando straightened himself in his hospital bed. Blood was rushing to his head, his eyes, growing wetter now, were fixed on Doctor Kelly. "Si," he said softly, looking at Maria, while his hand stretched to touch hers.

Doctor Kelly reached over and grabbed Armando's cigarettes off the bedside table. He then said in a powerful voice, "If you want to be around to see them, Armando, you must stop smoking today! **Not tomorrow! Not next week! TODAY!**" Armando smiled meekly, and nodded, as his hand finally reached and held his wife's.

Observing this from a short distance away Herman thought, *it is as if heaven is in this room.*

Cardiac disorders that Herman followed with Dr. Kelly that were particularly interesting, included patients with coronary artery disease and endocarditis. Herman treated such patients while they were in acute distress and followed them later in the cardiology clinic. Throughout his cardiac medicine rotation, Herman saw how interconnected one subspecialty was with other subspecialty areas. He remembered how the management of Mr. Carmine's atrial fibrillation of the heart may have contributed to a hemorrhagic stroke. Herman liked motivating patients to lose weight, stop smoking and become more active. He knew it had a positive impact on many cardiac illnesses. When a patient was having a cardiac arrest, Herman, while barking orders to attempt to get the patient resuscitated, felt the energy, drama, and trauma of a code blue. The adrenaline of the situation was like running for a touchdown but saving a patient's life exceeded any accomplishment on the gridiron.

✦　✦　✦

Psychiatry was Herman's next rotation with Doctor John McCarthy, who graduated from Villanova University with a degree in biology. After completing his four-year active-duty tour in the Navy, Dr. McCarthy graduated from Georgetown University Medical School and then did a residency in psychiatry at Walter Reed Medical Center. John practiced with a group of three psychiatrists and two psychologists. During Herman's rotation, his inpatients consisted of those suffering from post-traumatic stress disorder (PTSD) due to trauma endured in combat. Also were patients with chemical dependency, bipolar disorder, schizoaffective disorders, and an unusual case of dissociative fugue. Many of the patients were veterans. Herman also observed many of Doctor McCarthy's patients in his office. Herman found that it was hard not to conclude that the stress of combat, living through the Great Depression, or living through life changes like divorce or termination of employment often manifested themselves in physical as well as mental health problems.

One patient, Mary Ellen, had served as a nurse in World War II aboard the aircraft carrier USS Enterprise, affectionately known as the **Big E.** Mary Ellen, who grew up as a daughter of a wealthy coal baron family, longed to see the world and escape from the boredom of Bluefield, West Virginia. So, after high school, Mary Ellen finished nursing school, enlisted in the Navy, and found herself taking care of sailors in the aircraft carrier's sick bay. Trauma routinely visited Mary Ellen on the ship, first in Pearl Harbor, where eight of her airmen were killed, making the Big E the first to receive casualties during the War. As the carrier went on the attack in the battle of Midway, Death became a regular visitor. The Big E was attacked so often the Japanese thought they had sunk her, only to find the next day she was still standing. The Big E earned the nickname "The Gray Ghost," after its sailors spread the rumor that the ship couldn't die.

Mary Ellen tried to wall herself from the tragedies all around her. One dark night near the Eastern Solomons something happened that cracked her protective shell like a squirrel eating an acorn. Mary Ellen had met thousands of young men aboard the USS Enterprise. As a nurse, she was an officer, ate in the officers' mess hall, and socialized occasionally with the doctors and other officers on board. But it was one young sailor, Tommy Sullivan, who worked on the deck navigating planes, who caught her attention. Tommy was from neighboring Princeton, West Virginia, not far from where Mary Ellen grew up in Bluefield, West Virginia. He was from a good family, but trouble was his constant shadow. If he did not enlist his parents feared, he would end up in jail. Mary Ellen saw something in Tommy that no one else did. She was not sure if it was his imagination, the twinkle in his eye, or his deep faith. Tommy had complete optimism that he and she would survive the War. He was half right.

Towards the end of the War, after the Big E had downed 911 Japanese planes and sunk 71 ships, a lone Japanese Kamikaze Zero flying in an ink dark night fell from the sky, hitting the Big E on her flight deck. At the same time, Tommy was walking to meet Mary Ellen on the ship's starboard bow. Tommy's body was burned into a gruesome mass of melting flesh from his head to his torso. Taken to the infirmary, Tommy could not see Mary Ellen, but he could hear her voice cracking, sobbing, trying to comfort him. But Death slowly led him away, over the Big E's bow to rest peacefully in the depths below. The trauma to Mary Ellen caused repeated hallucinations. Images of his torn face and delusions that Tommy was still alive manifested themselves, causing Mary Ellen to experience uncontrollable schizoaffective disorder symptoms. One night such an episode brought Mary Ellen into Walter Reed's Emergency Room and admission to the psychiatric floor. Every cell in Herman's body was sensitive to her negative prognosis and hopeful her mood disorder drugs would bring her some comfort.

Another patient having a condition also borne out of the trauma suffered during the War was equally tragic. Andrew Brown was admitted through the Emergency Room to the psych floor with the unusual symptoms of hallucinations, delusion, and assuming the identity of a different person. Andrew was from Groton, Connecticut near the naval submarine base. Caught with patriotic fervor after Pearl Harbor, he entered the Army and fought first in Northern Africa and then in Sicily as a grunt infantry soldier. He almost made it through the War unscathed, until he faced a booby trap as he entered a villa looking for German soldiers, who were sent to help the Italians. The blast ripped off his left arm and cost him his right eye. Andrew went first to Brooks Army General Hospital in Fort Sam Houston for rehabilitation before being discharged. After leaving Brooks, Andrew struggled, living in halfway houses, and going to the VA for treatment. He was surviving though until a car backfired, causing Andrew to leave Texas, move to Washington D.C., where his folks lived, and to assume the identity of a naval officer in charge of a submarine built in Groton, Connecticut.

Herman listened attentively as Doctor McCarthy began recording Andrew's medical history. Herman discovered that Andrew's experience with a backfiring of a car was a traumatic event that caused Andrew to remember his previous boobytrap event that occurred in Italy. This caused Andrew to take flight and delude himself that he was a former submarine officer. His disorder, dissociative fugue, was rare. When delusions appear to be serious enough, patients like Andrew sometimes take on a new identity requiring that they be admitted for psychiatric treatment.

Herman then did a rotation in Nephrology with Doctor Gottlieb. Dr. Gottlieb was originally from Germany. His family left after the First World War and settled in Alexandria, Virginia. Doctor Gottlieb had wire-rim glasses and short white hair on the sides of his head. He walked with a slight limp from polio he contracted when he was a child in Frankfurt, Germany. Some of the patients Herman followed during this rotation had chronic kidney disease, kidney stones, nephritis, and blood in the urine.

One patient, Jack Reardon, who served in the Navy on a destroyer escorting ships that were ferrying troops to England for the D-Day invasion of Germany, Herman could not forget. Jack came into the ER in pain, vomiting, and had a high temperature. He was shaking like a reed in a windstorm. Summoned to the emergency room, Herman and Doctor Gottlieb examined him. Analyzing his urine, they noticed blood swirling in the glass container. Doctor Gottlieb ordered an x-ray, which revealed kidney stones. Mr. Reardon was discharged after a few hours and given a prescription for pain with a screen to catch the kidney stones for later examination. Given all the distress he presented when he arrived in the emergency room, Hermann was glad that the diagnosis and treatment plan were quickly determined.

✧ ✧ ✧

A Calling to Pursue

After Christmas, Herman rotated to what he knew would be his favorite subspecialty, infectious disease, with Doctor Bennett. Dr. Bennett was a tall slender female about 45 years old, with curly blond hair, blue eyes, and dimples, whose serious demeanor often was broken with a broad smile whenever she saw something pleasant. Herman was quick to mention his long-term interest in infectious disease, which went from the Spanish Flu pandemic and his grandfather's death to his work with Doctor Spencer in Charlotte, North Carolina.

"Jake, he is one smart guy, funny, with a strong set of principles. You do not want to cross him. I remember him well. We were together at the Marine Corps Officer Candidate School at Quantico, Virginia," she reminisced, showing Herman her wide smile as she recalled fond memories of Doctor Jake Spencer.

"So, you're a Marine too?"

"Yes. Semper Fidelis! I joined because of my father, who served as a Marine Captain and saw action along with 6000 other jarheads in the Battle of Guadalcanal. It was a critical time in World War II, marking the first time the United States went from defensive to offensive operations against the Japanese. It showed the importance of taking quick action, and the willingness of the Fleet Marine Force to attack when the rest of our ground troops were still in training. My dad received the Purple Heart. He was one of 1152 leathernecks who perished during their intense amphibious landing and fighting in the steaming tropical jungle on the island. From my family and the Marines, I got my resolve to take quick decisive action to stop the spread of infections, and the steel to fight these creatures."

Dr. Bennett added, "We see a lot of bugs here at Walter Reed - viruses, bacteria, parasites, fungi - causing a cornucopia of the world's communicable diseases. Do you know why?"

"It is because patients admitted to Walter Reed Hospital are soldiers and government officials who travel the world," Herman responded.

"Yes, travel. If the travel is slow, like on a ship as in the past, there is a strong possibility that for anyone arriving in the US by boat, the infection they have might have lost its potency. Or the traveler may be cured or dead, leaving the pathogen no new host to grab onto. With quicker plane travel, however, bugs can spread from an infected passenger on the plane or at his or her destination through skin contact, airborne particles, or by touching a surface before the pathogens are defeated. When the infected person enters an airport and then transmits the infection to others, sometimes it causes an epidemic. If it spreads beyond a country, it could lead to a pandemic," she explained while motioning for Herman to join her on her rounds.

The first patient was Bill Cardinal, a Navy pilot, who had meningitis, which Herman learned could be caused by a virus, bacteria, parasite, or fungus. Bill was vomiting, had headaches, and a fever. Doctor Bennett and Herman put on protective gear to enter his isolation room. When Doctor Bennett showed light into his eyes, Bill blinked and pulled away. Doctor Bennett looked at the chart and asked Mr. Cardinal if he had had contact with anyone like a child who had a fever. She then examined his neck for stiffness, looked at the rash on his skin, listened to his heart rate, and noted the high temperature that the nurse had recorded. Doctor Bennett then ordered a blood culture, a complete blood count, and a chest x-ray. After that she took a glass from her pocket and rolled it over his rash, noting that it did not fade under the pressure of the glass tube.

"Mr. Cardinal, I ordered some tests, and I can assure you we will get to the bottom of this. I think you have bacterial meningitis, but the tests will confirm it, and then we will get you some medicine to restore your health. Thank you for your service to the country. Did you see any action?" she asked.

"Yes, I was involved in several flights over Midway in the Pacific before being shot down. Luckily our Navy boys were nearby and scooped me out of the drink," he replied, feeling his chest with air. Doctor Bennett reassured Mr. Cardinal she would be back after receiving his test results. She held his hand tight, looked him straight in the eye, and mentioned that her dad had fought at Guadalcanal, which drew nods of acceptance between them.

Doctor Bennett and Herman went to visit other patients: a middle-aged man with hepatitis, an elderly overweight woman with a urinary tract infection, a child with strep throat, and a lady in her sixties who had contracted a fungus nail infection that spread throughout her body. After several weeks of rotation, Doctor Elizabeth Bennett praised Herman for his attention to detail, probing questions, and the extensive reading he did to understand each patient's condition. She welcomed him to apply for a fellowship in infectious disease, and she assured him that he would receive favorable treatment.

Herman's last rotation was in Neurology with Doctor Russell, a short man with a pointed triangular chin, mustache, and brown hair, who graduated from George Washington University and the University of Virginia Medical School. He often reminded medical students that the UVA School of Medicine was established by Thomas Jefferson. Herman found his rotation with Doctor Ned Russell fast and fascinating. Herman read extensively to be better able to answer questions regarding the diagnosis, treatment, and, most important to Herman, how to prevent the illness of patients. The contrast was stark between the high energy of Ned, who often took the stairs two at a time, and his patients lying either unconscious or slowly moving or speaking. Some of his patients were stroke victims. Others suffered seizures or had encephalitis. There were also patients with Huntington's Disease and Parkinson's Disease.

One patient was particularly interesting, Anthony Mancini, from the Bronx. Mr. Mancini had ALS, Amyotrophic Lateral Sclerosis, which was first discovered, Herman found out, by a French neurologist in 1869. ALS became more widely known however when it ended the career of one of baseball's beloved players, Lou Gehrig. Herman learned that the disease was caused by a mutation in a gene. In about ten percent of ALS cases, it is passed down from one parent to a child. Doctor Russell, in a compassionate manner, reassured Tony, "We confirmed the diagnosis of Amyotrophic Lateral Sclerosis. We will support you in every way we can, when your weakness caused by ALS increases, we will be understanding, and caring of you and your family. We will provide the most up-to-date medical therapy. We will, if the need arises, make you comfortable, as we follow the progression of the disease."

Tony absorbed the information without showing much personal negative emotion. Rather he felt for his family and made a special effort to console his wife Marie and his son, who were at his bedside. Tony then said, "Doc, as bad as this is, I'm glad to be in the company of Lou Gehrig. I remember one hot day in July, sitting in the bleachers at Yankee Stadium with my son Johnny. Seeing Lou with his friend and teammate Babe Ruth at his side. They were standing at a microphone while 60 thousand fans waited to hear Lou speak. I can still see a solitary crow sitting on top of the flag-pole in Centerfield; smell the hot dog that was smothered with mustard from the pot-bellied large man sitting next to us; and hear the crowd growing silent in anticipation - as Lou cleared his throat to speak. Lou Gehrig said with honest appreciation, with a pow-erful voice that was breaking up with emotion, silence, and more emotion. Lou said he considered himself the luckiest man on the face of the earth to have played with the New York Yankees.... Today, Doc, I too, consider myself also very lucky. Lucky! Yes, lucky! **You betcha lucky** - to have such a wonderful family!" he proclaimed, as Marie and Johnny hugged him from all sides.

As Ned and Herman walked away, Herman put one hand on his chin, like he was holding it up, while contemplating what he just witnessed. *A man with a deadly diagnosis grateful for what he had, not what he didn't have.*

Herman finished his rotations, applied for his fellowship in infectious disease, and anxiously awaited graduation. Betsy, Jacob, Margarita and Judith were seated in the auditorium at Walter Reed General Hospital on the last Friday in June 1946, when Herman received his medical residency Certificate of Completion.

They listened to the solemn words of Major General Doctor Norman Kirk, Surgeon General of the United States Army.

"Today we are gathered here to commemorate the graduation of our finest doctors, who have endured rigorous studies and long stressful hours caring for our government leaders and soldiers. I've treated men and women who were blown apart in battle. I have watched the eyes of the fatally wounded fade to unconsciousness and death. I have experienced a military ravaged by tropical diseases. I can tell you, if America is going to stand tall as a beacon for freedom, we will need doctors like these we celebrate here today. We need the best and the brightest to care for our soldiers, sailors, marines, air force, and coast guard more than we need bullets and armor. We will need expert physicians to patch up broken bodies, mend busted minds, and fight diseases like the Spanish Flu that killed more men than bullets in the First World War. We will need sterling doctors with spines of steel to sustain and build trust. Our military personnel must believe that we in the medical profession will do everything possible, and **I mean everything,** to restore the health of those who have sacrificed so much for this country!"

✧ ✧ ✧

Being accepted into the infectious disease fellowship was important to Herman. Learning about infectious illnesses was paramount ever since his grandfather died because of the pandemic of 1918 when Herman was just five years old. Herman knew that fellowship slots were very competitive. Given the prejudices that existed in medicine, he knew he needed a champion working on his behalf. Herman reached out and called Jake Spencer MD, Chief of Pathology at Charlotte Memorial Hospital, where Herman had worked when he was in high school and in college. "Dr. Spencer, this is Herman Jackson."

"Hello Herman, how are you? I hadn't heard from you for a while, so I thought perhaps you had dropped out of medical school and we're playing pro football somewhere," Jake responded. Then Jake added, "Just kidding."

"No, those days are behind me. I am at Walter Reed General Hospital in Washington D.C. in the third year of my Internal Medicine Residency," Herman responded, realizing he should have done a better job staying in touch.

"So, what are your plans?" Doctor Spencer asked.

"I would like to do a fellowship, preferably at Walter Reed in infectious disease," Herman said.

"That would be good for you. There is a growing need for that kind of specialist. Viruses, bacteria, and other bugs are becoming more prevalent because of dense populations, more people traveling around the globe, and the organisms mutating faster than we can develop vaccines and drugs to stop them. You will be respected and sought after for your expertise, which will matter more than your race. I believe I know the director of your fellowship program. Is it still Doctor Elizabeth Bennett? I met her when we were both at Quantico at the Marine OCS School."

"Yes, she is still here," Herman said. "Could you be one of my references?"

"I would be honored."

"Thanks, Doctor Spencer."

"After all these years, just call me Jake."

Chapter Sixteen

FELLOWSHIP IN
INFECTIOUS DISEASE

HERMAN WAS THRILLED that he was accepted for an infectious disease fellowship with Elizabeth Bennett M.D., and that based on his previous experience and the recommendation of Jake Spencer M.D., he could complete it in one year. Fellowship training was like an extended rotation only more intense. One got exposed to a great variety of patients. Walter Reed, being the flagship Hospital of the military and government, received patients from all over the United States and the world, including those who had served active duty abroad during World War I & II. This was especially important for an infectious disease fellow because many of the patients cared for were exposed to pathogens, viruses, bacteria, parasites, and fungi that one might not see in normal practice in a community hospital. All it would take is one patient returning infected from a trip out of the country to start an epidemic, if not handled properly.

For instance, one patient, Robert Schiffer, after serving in the Pacific, returned to the states after stopping off in Australia. A mosquito, infected with the dengue virus, attached itself to him.

Robert did not have any symptoms for a while. Then when he went to the ER at Walter Reed Mr. Schiffer had a high fever, headaches, swollen lymph glands, skin rash, and could not stop vomiting. He was admitted and placed in an isolation room. Because the infectious disease was suspected, Herman responded Saturday night around eleven o'clock. Herman ordered medications, blood tests, and increased fluids. He observed that Robert was bleeding from his nose and worried that his disease might progress to dengue shock syndrome. Before going any further, Herman contacted Dr. Bennett to get advice on treating Mr. Schiffer. Dr. Bennett said, "There was no specific treatment for the fever other than to make the patient comfortable, use tepid sponge baths, and instead of aspirin give acetaminophen, the recently approved pain medicine by the FDA." Eventually, after the weekend, Mr. Shiffer's fever subsided, and he was on the road to recovery as well as now being immune to one of the dengue viruses. Since he was still vulnerable to the two other dengue viruses, he was instructed to stay away from places like Mexico or the Caribbean Islands, where those viruses could be present.

Several patients Herman saw during his fellowship had diseases like measles, diphtheria, and tetanus, which could have been prevented had the patient been vaccinated against these pathogens in childhood.

Dr. Bennett instructed, "Part of the responsibility of infectious disease physicians and pediatricians, as well as other experts in public health, is to convince parents of the benefits of vaccination in preventing illnesses and stopping their transmission to others. Unless we achieve herd immunity with at least 60% of the children being vaccinated or having antibodies from a previous infection, outbreaks of illness will occur. The costs of vaccines are minimal compared to the pain, suffering, loss of income, and disruption to the economy when an epidemic happens. Not all people support vaccinations. There was an uprising in Delaware in 1926 over the State's vaccine mandate. There is an element of American culture, called 'rugged individualism,' that is opposed to anyone telling us what to do. Many African American mothers are against vaccination, which may be due to a shortage of Negro doctors to convince them, a lack of disposable income, fear of complications or being used for research "

Herman finished his fellowship in record time due to his knowledge and dedication. Dr. Bennett knew physicians of color were scarce and needed in their communities. She agreed that Herman had completed his requirements for taking the Boards in Infectious Disease, which Herman passed on his first try.

Chapter Seventeen

HOMEWARD BOUND

HERMAN HAD A big decision to make. He could go to a big academic medical center consulting on infectious disease patients and doing research, or he could return to Charlotte and start a practice in internal medicine and do consultations on infectious diseases when requested. He also had to complete his obligations as a Captain in the United States Army Reserves. In deciding, Herman was influenced by his parents, who were getting older, and the needs of his Brooklyn community in the Third Ward of Charlotte. He was well-known in the area because of his days running track in high school and football in college, as well as his years teaching history at the Third Ward High School. Herman was confident that he could build a practice and could get on the staff of Good Samaritan Hospital, which was built and operated for colored folks in Charlotte. His mind made up; Herman decided to go back home. The Jacksons bought a brick home on Beatties Ford Road which had three bedrooms and an attic big enough to be converted for Herman's parents to live in. As expected, they were welcomed back by many friends. Herman opened an office just down the street from his home. Good Samaritan Hospital wasted no time in admitting him to their staff and naming him the Director of Infection Control and Prevention.

In the 1900's sick or injured North Carolinians were cared for primarily at home. Contagious illnesses, however, often arrived on ships. Therefore, facilities were erected to quarantine incoming seamen who were ill. The same hospital beds were used to treat patients with malaria or other infectious diseases. One of the first, Mount Tirzah Hospital, was built in 1835 in Wilmington, North Carolina.

Further evolution of hospitals in North Carolina rested with religious organizations. Good Samaritan Hospital was an example of such spiritual intervention. It was built in the middle of West Hill Street between Mint and Garden in Charlotte's Third Ward. It was the first privately funded independent Hospital in North Carolina constructed for colored folks. Good Samaritan Hospital's beginnings were rooted in the beliefs of the Episcopal Church and the determined efforts of Jane Renwick Wilkes. Mrs. Wilkes was active in the Saint Peter's Episcopal Church, which had a philosophy of spiritual and physical healing. Mrs. Wilkes and other ladies of the church saw the need for a hospital, through their nursing work for Confederate soldiers wounded during the war. Mrs. Wilkes and the Saint Peter's Episcopal Church ladies club called the Blue Bees went on to raise funds to build a four-room hospital for White people called Saint Peter's Hospital that was completed in 1878. Then the Episcopal Church, with the untiring fundraising help of Mrs. Wilkes, suggested that Saint Michael's Chapel and Good Samaritan Hospital be built for the colored community. The Hospital was completed in 1891. In 1925 a major addition was added, making the hospital a hundred-bed facility with the latest equipment. The hospital prospered as did the rest of Charlotte, but in the late 1930s, it became increasingly difficult for some church-sponsored hospitals to thrive. In 1940 Saint Peter's Hospital closed when Charlotte Memorial Hospital opened. Good Samaritan struggled but continued its mission with support from the colored community.

✧ ✧ ✧

Although Good Samaritan received high marks for its nursing care from the community it served, many still thought of it as a place where colored people went to die. Some patients who came to Herman for outpatient minor injuries or ailments were hesitant to go to Good Samaritan Hospital when they needed hospitalization. Herman did not like losing patients who felt the care at Good Samaritan Hospital was not as good as other facilities. Moreover, he had not appreciated the stigma of being "not good enough" to be a member of Charlotte Memorial Hospital. Ever since he first heard the stories of his grandfather who endured the whip and ran to freedom, Herman did not shy away from a fight - not on the gridiron, and not now. Faced with discrimination that affected the health of his patients and the livelihood of his family, Herman chose to be a leader.

One afternoon in September, Herman sent a letter to Charlotte Memorial Hospital requesting an application for admission to the medical staff with privileges in internal medicine and infectious disease. When Herman received the application, he filled it out. He had Johnson Smith University, University of Michigan, Meharry Medical School, and Walter Reed Army Hospital send transcripts of his grades and evidence of his degrees to Charlotte Memorial Hospital. A month went by without any acknowledgment that Charlotte Memorial Hospital had received his application or was processing it. Herman followed up with a letter asking Charlotte Memorial if they needed further information and still heard nothing. Next, he called the office and spoke to the medical staff secretary, who informed Herman that his application was on hold until Herman submitted evidence that he was a member of the Mecklenburg County Medical Society. Herman then followed up and talked to the Medical Society to get an application. He completed the application and mailed it in with his check, but when he did not hear anything, Herman contacted the Medical Society. It was then that Herman was told the racist truth: the Medical Society did not admit Negro physicians.

The news hit him hard. How could the Medical Society be so prejudicial? The Medical Society members knew that physicians, by sharing information with colleagues and attending conferences, obtained knowledge that benefited both physicians and patients. To deny membership in the Medical Society and so prevent a black physician from becoming an attending staff member at Charlotte Memorial Hospital was tantamount to not only stigmatizing physicians of color but also diminishing the healthcare system that the Negro community depended upon. Moreover, by lowering healthcare services for colored people, the White physicians were ensuring the vulnerability of their own White population based on the law of the weakest link. That law implied that when one group is more susceptible to communicable diseases due to living in unhealthy conditions, and/or having little access to quality affordable healthcare, it leaves other groups with better living arrangements and/or complete access to healthcare vulnerable to the same diseases. For once an epidemic starts in one segment of the population that suffers from poor healthcare, the infection can and will be transmitted to those in good health who are not immune.

Race was being used to treat people differently when it came to a basic right like health care, even though in the Declaration of Independence it is recorded:

> *We hold these truths to be self-evident, that all men are created equal, that they are endowed by their Creator with certain unalienable Rights, that among these are Life, Liberty, and the pursuit of Happiness.*

Herman knew from history that "race" was a word used in the United States ever since Dutch traders in 1619 sold the first African slaves in Jamestown, Virginia. The word continued to be used even after the passage of the 13th Amendment, which officially ended slavery, in 1865. The issue of using race to deny admitting physicians of color to membership in their Association was first discussed at the American Medical Association, AMA, after the Civil War, in 1868. At the time, the AMA's Ethics

Committee, following the AMA's National Convention, was debating the question of whether they should admit female physicians. The passage of the Fourteenth Amendment granted citizenship to all persons born or naturalized in the United States, including formerly enslaved people. The Amendment provided all citizens with equal protection under the laws. In accordance with the spirit of the 14th Amendment, the AMA's Ethics Committee recommended that female physicians not be denied admission to the AMA because of their sex. The full body of the AMA, however, did not want to tackle such a divisive issue as race so close to the end of the Civil War. They wanted southern physicians to join the AMA organization. As a result, the AMA decided to leave the matter of admission of physicians based on sex or race up to the local medical societies.

In doing his research for planning his attack on the discriminatory practices of the Mecklenburg Medical Society, Herman dug deeper into the history of the AMA. He found that the national AMA organization, to preserve tranquility between their northern and southern factions, baked institutional racism into the healthcare system by trading away the civil rights of Negro physicians. Much in the same way the founders of the United States, although proclaiming all men are created equal, allowed slavery to continue to form the union of the 13 northern and southern colonies.

In 1870 the issue of equality was brought up again at the AMA's annual meeting. Battle lines were drawn as both the all-White Medical Society of D.C. and the integrated delegations from the Freedmen Hospital and Howard University sought admission at the convention. Leading the integrated delegations was Robert Rayburn from Howard University Medical College. Dr. Rayburn was a White former Union Army officer and military surgeon. The integrated organizations demanded that physicians of color who met all the requirements for admission not be denied based solely on the color of their skin. Nonetheless, the AMA voted to deny admission to the integrated delegations, siding with the segregated D.C. Medical Society. The AMA's strategy of allowing the local medical societies to set the admission requirements was also played out in Mecklenburg County, North Carolina, when the Medical Society denied Herman admission to their organization. Such efforts of blatant discrimination caught the eye of civil rights activists, including the leaders of the NAACP.

Chapter Eighteen

THE NIGHTINGALE SINGS

GEORGE ANDERSON, CEO of First National Bank, knew something was not right when his secretary, Mrs. Donahue interrupted his meeting in the mahogany-paneled boardroom to say his wife was on the phone. George took the call in his private office. "Grace, what's the matter? How is Carol? Okay, I understand, but is her fever getting worse? Is her temperature back up again? Still, undulating up and down? This is too many days of illness," he said with concern.

"Carol feels a lot worse. Her temperature is 103. She is very weak and tired. She says her knees, as well as her shoulders, are hurting. And she is throwing up," Grace Anderson said, trying to catch her breath.

"Call an ambulance, and I will meet you at Charlotte Memorial Hospital."

George, having served in the Army as a captain before the War, knew how important it was to make quick decisions when one's health was on the line. He abruptly ended his luncheon meeting, left the Bank, and rushed to the Hospital. Carol, with her mother sitting next to her in the ambulance, arrived at Charlotte Memorial Hospital at 12:30 pm. She was then accompanied by two ambulance attendants, a triage nurse firing questions, and a registration clerk obtaining her insurance information. Once inside, nurses transferred Carol to a hospital stretcher and pushed her into a cubicle as a curtain was drawn.

Next, more questions from a physician while a nurse started intravenous fluids. Carol drifted into a confused state, her eyes looking away from overhead piercing lights, her nose was bathed by pungent smells of alcohol, and her ears were drowning from nearby voices, stretchers with squeaky wheels, and ambulances arriving. After completing her history and physical, the ER physician requested Carol be admitted. Grace, holding her only child's hand, was relieved when an orderly brought Carol to a quiet private room on the third floor. They settled in and waited for what seemed like an eternity as nurses took vital signs, refreshed the water picture, and reassured Mrs. Anderson that Doctor Cashman, Carol's personal physician, would be in during his daily rounds.

Carol was a slender girl, 23 years old, with short blond hair, hazel eyes, high cheekbones, and usually a generous smile. Today her lips were tight and worried, her smile wiped away because of her fever. After graduating from the private distinguished Hotchkiss School in Lakeville, Connecticut, and Queens University in Charlotte, Carol applied to go to veterinary school at Duke University and North Carolina State University at Raleigh. She was patiently waiting to hear from these schools, which were competitive to get into. Because of her love of animals, Carol made repeated trips to the family's hobby farm outside of Charlotte, in Monroe County, North Carolina. The ranch had horses, cattle, and a pet goat.

Grace Anderson was a socialite, active at the Covenant Presbyterian Church and at charitable functions of different stripes in Charlotte. She came from a wealthy family that had a farm outside of Louisville, Kentucky, where they raised racehorses. Grace's mother inherited money from her parents' coal mining business in Kentucky and West Virginia.

George Anderson arrived at Carol's room around one. He was a tall man with good posture, lean as a wooden stud, with light brown hair. His trajectory to be president of the First Union Bank began with his attending Avon Old Farms, a private school in Avon, Connecticut, followed by degrees in economics at Duke University where he also ran track and a master's degree in business from The Wharton School at the University of Pennsylvania. After a brief tour in the Army, George began his corporate career in banking and playing golf at the Charlotte Country Club.

George paced in front of Carol's hospital window. He looked at his watch repeatedly, anxious for Doctor Cashman to arrive, not used to the experience of waiting or their child being ill. Grace sat on the edge of the bed, nervously wringing her hands, and fidgeting with her pearl necklace.

Doctor John Cashman was short, with thin shoulders, a dimpled chin, and thick, tortoise rim glasses covering tired eyes. He graduated medical school from Emory in Atlanta and did his Internal Medicine Residency at the University Medical Center in Charleston, South Carolina. He came from a family whose vast wealth derived from being part owner of a gypsum manufacturing company. Although Cashman's older brothers were athletic, John preferred a sedentary life of reading and schoolwork. While his brothers went into business with support from their father, John planned to become a doctor. Throughout his life, John Cashman lived in the shadow of his brothers, which made him feel inferior. John was propelled by his ambition to succeed financially in his chosen profession, despite his average medical intellect.

Doctor Cashman admitted many patients, even those whose condition could have been better cared for at home. Because of his busy practice he often seemed overwhelmed, hassled, and not tentative about the details of treating patients. So, it was not surprising to the nurses on Three South that Dr. Cashman was late seeing Carol Anderson. And when he did show up at 4 pm, he did not give prompt feedback to her parents about her condition, or his plan for treatment.

Carol's condition continued to deteriorate. Her 103-degree temperature showed no signs of retreating, but it did undulate significantly. Overnight her sheets were wet from perspiration, and her knees, arms, and shoulders ached. She vomited and had a minimal appetite. Nurses on the floor made extensive notes documenting Carol's condition. Doctor Cashman, perhaps because he was too busy with his many patients, did not take aggressive action. Neither did the junior year resident, Lee Maybury. Dr. Mayberry was quite overweight. He had a strange propensity to think any medical condition was a cause for an extensive GI workup. Rachel, the Three South head nurse, was particularly concerned and contemplated going above Doctor Cashman, in an unusual move to request of her Nursing Director that the Chief of Medicine should intervene. George and Grace Anderson were doubly concerned. Carol was their only child. They were used to being in control, commanding action to their requests, but this situation seemed unmanageable.

George saw physicians on the floor coming in and out of rooms with an air of confidence about them. He became frantic, asking Rachel repeatedly, "Have you heard from Cashman yet?"

When Doctor Cashman did appear, he did not raise the Andersons' confidence in him. He examined Carol and gave the charge nurse orders for medications and blood tests, but he did not answer Carol's parents' questions regarding what was going on with their child.

✧ ✧ ✧

Across Town at Good Samaritan Hospital

Although the equipment was older, and the rooms in the corridors could use some fresh paint, Herman enjoyed practicing at Good Samaritan Hospital. Physicians joked in the doctor's lounge, talked about sports, and were supportive of one another. They often asked Herman for advice or requested he look at one of their patients. Herman received many consults, chaired the Infectious Disease Committee, and worked with the designated infection control nurse giving advice on isolation, probability of transmission of disease, and prevention measures.

Herman was an avid reader. He published articles in the Journal of Infectious Disease, which covered research on the diagnosis and treatment of infectious diseases. He paid close attention to the literature relating to the microbes that caused disease in persons with immune system disorders. Herman read the Tropical Disease Bulletin, which was a source of news regarding epidemics occurring around the world. To Herman, it seemed that outbreaks were increasing as more people traveled to tropical areas, where they were close to wild animals who often acted as hosts for viruses, bacteria, or parasites. All these illnesses had the potential to migrate to the United States.

Outside of work, Herman was active in the community. Often, he attended sporting events in familiar surroundings like the Third Ward High School and Johnson Smith University. He was a member of the Alpha Phi Alpha fraternity, an officer in the local YMCA, and a member of the Boule, a civic-minded organization of business leaders.

The tranquility of his medical and personal life, however, like an errant baseball breaking a window, was about to be shattered.

✧　✧　✧

Charlotte Memorial Hospital

George Anderson was a man who demanded action when the situation warranted. He was not about to fiddle around talking to a middleman about his concerns. He would take them to the top dog. He knew the President of the Hospital, Todd Allen, from serving on the Hospital's Board, and they were both members of Rotary International. He told his wife he was going to see Todd.

At the same time, Rachel, the head nurse on the Third Floor Unit, was going to lunch. As Rachel got on the elevator, in a low voice she said, "Hello, Doctor Spencer."

Jake could sense that Rachel, who he knew from their service on the Infection Control Committee, was not her usual self. Her skin was pale, and she had a worried look plastered on her face. When they exited the elevator he said, "Rachel, I do not want to be nosey, but is there something wrong?"

Rachel looked around to see if anyone was listening, and replied, "Yes."

"I am just going to pick something up at the cafeteria. Do you want to get something and join me in my office for lunch?"

"Yes! Umm, yes! I will meet you there," Rachel said sharply with dull emotion from straight lips.

With a tuna fish sandwich in her hand, Rachel sat down in Doctor Spencer's office. She glanced at his desk cluttered with files, journals, and reference books. Rachel was apprehensive about talking to Doctor Spencer concerning Carol Anderson. There might be negative consequences for not following the usual chain of command when a nurse raises concern over a physician's treatment of one of his patients. Ever since Rachel entered nursing school and a nursing cap was placed upon her head, she felt a strong pull to do what was best for her patients. It was the motivation behind her passion for training her staff. She could be outspoken when the situation called for action, asking questions, or expressing her feelings - like she was about to do now with conviction. Like so many of her nursing colleagues at Charlotte Memorial Hospital, Rachel was driven by the professional part of the Nightingale Pledge. She lived by the command to *"devote yourself to the welfare of those committed to your care."*

"So, what is it?" Jake began, as he sat next to Rachel and took a sip from his black coffee. Rachel looked at the man bigger than life, yet totally interested in what could be bothering her. His large frame bent forward towards her as an invitation for Rachel to confidently open her mind and heart to this Doctor. Preceding anything they would say was an imprimatur of trust - knowing they both shared similar values.

"There is a patient on my floor who has a fever of unknown origin. She's vomiting, with joint pain, and her parents, George and Grace Anderson are worried about their daughter's treatment. Perhaps her physician, Doctor Cashman, is busy, but he does not seem to be too concerned," Rachel explained with a rigid, tight face, but compassion in her voice.

"Has he consulted anyone?" Doctor Spencer asked.

"No."

Doctor Spencer and Rachael locked eyes on one another. The silence that followed communicated more than the words that were just spoken.

"Rachel, I appreciate you sharing this with me. I will investigate it, and keep our conversation confidential," he replied, rising like a whale coming to the surface.

Doctor Spencer was aware that Doctor Cashman had a large practice. He heard through the grapevine that patients and their families often complained to nurses that he seemed aloof or abrupt. Communications were not optimal. Doctor Spencer, who served on the Hospital's Quality Assurance Committee, had recently sat through a medical staff presentation on the importance of listening to a patient as a means of establishing rapport and improving patient satisfaction. Although Jake was removed from direct patient contact as a pathologist, he had a reputation as a champion of patient rights and was fiercely loyal to the Hospital and the nurses.

✧ ✧ ✧

Dr. Spencer had a feeling that the patient Rachel described may have an infectious disease. The infectious disease physician at Charlotte Memorial was on vacation. He also knew George Anderson was President of the First National Bank and on the Hospital's board. Mr. Anderson would demand and deserve the best possible care. Jake wondered if this might be the best time to kill two birds with one stone.

I will bring in the best infectious disease physician in Charlotte to see the patient, and I will break the race barrier at the same time. To do this I need to see Todd Allen and ask him to give Herman Jackson M.D. temporary privileges at the parents' request. Then I will get that weasel, son of a bitch Cashman, to write the consult order; or I will break his arm!

Having decided, Jake walked briskly out of his office, ignoring a request from the lab technologist to speak to him. He headed to Administration, and a confrontation if need be. When Doctor Spencer arrived at the Administration Office, his feet sunk into the plush carpet. He could not help but notice the leather chairs and expensive-looking artwork on the walls.

"Please let Mr. Allen know that Jake Spencer wants to see him. It's important," Jake requested.

Ms. Martin, a slim lady with brown hair and wearing a blue suit dress, peered over her black-framed reading glasses, and replied, "Mr. Allen is on a call. When he gets off, I will check for you."

Just then the door to Administration opened, and Jake recognized George Anderson from Rotary International Club. "What's up George, how is the family?" Jake asked, faking ignorance.

"Well, Grace and I are fine, but my daughter is in your Hospital and not doing well," Mr. Anderson replied in a low voice with a blank chalky look on his face.

Jake motioned for the two of them to step into the corridor for more privacy. "What floor is your daughter on?" he asked.

"She is on the third floor. Doctor Cashman is her private physician, but I'm not sure he has any idea what the hell is wrong with Carol, who has a fever, is sweating, and throwing up constantly," George replied.

"Sounds like Carol may have an unusual infectious disease, George. I know one of the best infectious disease physician specialists in all of North Carolina. He used to work for me," Jake said reassuringly.

"Jake, we suggested to Doctor Cashman that he bring in someone to look at Carol, but he was reluctant. Said, 'Let's see how she does first.'"

"Well, I can talk to Cashman in a manner he won't refuse. First, we must ask Todd Allen, at your request, to grant temporary privileges to the infectious disease specialist, Doctor Herman Jackson, to see Carol," Jake instructed.

"Sounds good. If you have time, can you talk to Mr. Allen with me?" George asked.

"I will make time," Jake said.

After they came back into the Administration offices, Jake asked Ms. Martin if Mr. Allen was off the phone or just taking a nap. Upon checking, she said in a monotone, "Mr. Allen will see you now."

Todd Allen was dressed impeccably in a gray suit. He resided in a luxurious office with a nice view, and with his degrees conspicuously gracing the wall behind his large desk, the top of which was empty. Todd had attended Duke University as an undergraduate and had received his master's degree from Vanderbilt University.

He was tall with closely cropped brown hair, wire-rimmed glasses, and a frown, showing his displeasure with the disruption of his routine. "Todd, George's daughter, Carol, is under the care of Doctor Cashman. George and his wife, Grace, would like an infectious disease specialist not on our staff to see their daughter," Doctor Spencer began.

"Well, why doesn't Doctor Cashman consult our specialist?" Mr. Allen replied.

"I do not know, Todd, I think he is temporarily out of town. George is requesting that you, as President, in accordance with our bylaws, grant temporary privileges to Herman Jackson, M.D.. Dr. Jackson is Board Certified in Internal Medicine, with a Fellowship in Infectious Disease. George wants Dr. Jackson to examine his daughter."

"Doctor Cashman will not like this intrusion on what he considers his prerogatives, Doctor Spencer," Allen replied. "You know that!"

"Todd, let me handle that; you just give the temporary privileges. I will get Cashman to write the consult request, and I will personally contact Doctor Jackson to get him over here this afternoon. No time to waste, Todd. You have the authority to make this decision. Now make it," Jake said, leaving no doubt he would not back down.

"Okay." Mr. Allen uttered, as his eyes showed his displeasure. He picked up the phone. "Ms. Martin, can you prepare temporary privileges for Herman Jackson, M.D. to examine and treat Carol Anderson for my signature."

"Thank you, Todd," George and Jake said, as they turned and left his office.

In the hallway, Jake said, "I will call Doctors Jackson and Cashman. George, I will call you this afternoon." Then Jake walked back to his office.

✧ ✧ ✧

Across Town in Doctor Jackson's Office

Herman was writing progress notes from treating patients when his nurse said that Doctor Spencer was on the phone. "I'll take it."

"Herman, I must ask you for a favor. There is a young lady over here with a fever of unknown origin who is not doing well. Her father is on our Board. Our CEO, Todd Allen, has agreed to give you temporary privileges if you would see this patient. I will get the consult request from Doctor Cashman, the attending physician. Can you come over right away?" Jake asked.

"Sure, Jake. I will reschedule my afternoon appointments. What's the girl's name, and where is she?" Herman asked.

"Her name is Carol Anderson, and she is in Room 310."

✧ ✧ ✧

Doctor Cashman's Office

Next Jake went to see Doctor Cashman in his office, which was in the Medical Staff Building next to the Hospital.

"John, hello. I can see that you are busy," Jake began.

"Well, this is a surprise," Doctor Cashman replied, knowing that Jake was rarely seen outside of the Hospital, except for the Christmas party, when Jake often played Santa Claus.

"John, I will get right to the point. You have a young lady, Carol Anderson, in room 310. I know the father, and he came to me concerned about his daughter. From what he told me, she may have some sort of infectious bug," Jake commented.

"Really, why didn't Mr. Anderson contact me about his daughter?" said Dr. Cashman, appearing upset.

"Listen, John, don't get your pants wet. I know an infectious disease specialist, probably the best in the State of North Carolina. All you need to do is call in the consult. He will see your patient, and give you, his advice. You will look like a hero," Jake said calmly, but forcefully.

"And if I don't?" Doctor Cashman retorted, raising his agitated voice. "John, you do not want to go there."

"This is highly inappropriate, Jake, for you to be interfering with a doctor-patient relationship."

"I am Chairman of the Hospital's Ethics Committee, and the family is upset at the management of their daughter's care. The father has already gone to Todd Allen, our President. Anderson is President of the First National Bank and on our Board. If you lose their child, a lawsuit will be the least of your troubles," Jake said, red-faced and glaring at Doctor Cashman.

"Okay, I will call in for the consultation. What is the doctor's name?"

"Herman Jackson M.D. Do it now. I will see that Dr. Jackson gets right over to see the patient," Jake said, as he waved goodbye.

✧ ✧ ✧

Herman pulled into the visitors' parking lot and entered the emergency room of Charlotte Memorial Hospital. Herman was wearing his long white doctor's coat with a stethoscope draped over his shoulders, like a sleeping reptile. A security guard asked where he was going.

"I must see a patient, Carol Anderson, in room 310, for a consultation. I am Doctor Jackson," Herman said, showing his identification. The guard called up to the third floor to confirm that a patient named Carol Anderson was in room 310 and that the nurse related they were expecting Doctor Jackson. Herman took the stairs two at a time up to the third floor, went into the nursing station, and asked to see the head nurse. Rachel was nearby and greeted Herman.

"I am here to see Carol Anderson in 310," he said.

Rachel grabbed Carol's medical record and handed it to Doctor Jackson. He looked at the physical, history, and progress notes. Doctor Cashman's were brief, and those of the nurses were extensive.

"Dr. Jackson, can I talk to you in private?" Rachel asked, leading him to her office, which was no bigger than a utility closet.

"Doctor Jackson, Carol has been running a fever of 103 since she arrived. She is not doing well. I fear she is slipping away," Rachel said.

Herman, with Rachel accompanying him, proceeded to room 310, put on his mask, and introduced himself to Carol, as well as her parents, explaining calmly his credentials and that Doctor Cashman had asked him to examine Carol. The parents were asked for additional history information. They were asked to wait in the floor lounge while Doctor Herman examined Carol. Herman went to the sink and washed his hands. He took her temperature, blood pressure, pulse, and respiratory rate. He examined her head, ears, eyes, nose, and mouth thoroughly. He listened to her heart and lungs carefully. He positioned his stethoscope on his neck while examining Carol's lymph nodes, abdomen, and other appropriate areas of her body. He examined her knees and elbows and asked if she was feeling pain in those areas.

In a calm, reassuring, confident voice, Herman continued to obtain more pertinent history, "So I hear you went to Queens University. I once ran in a track meet there. It's a beautiful campus. I read the nurse's notes before coming in here. Is it true that you have an interest in veterinary medicine?"

"Yes," Carol said, clearing her throat as Herman poured a glass of water for her. "I have applied to two schools and am waiting to hear from Duke and North Carolina University in Raleigh."

"That's good. With all the farms outside of Charlotte, we are going to need more veterinarians," Herman replied.

Smiling now, Carol said, "We have a family farm in Monroe County."

"I see. Do you go there often?" Herman asked casually, thinking the answer might be important.

"Yes, I have been going there often over the last three months. Ever since we bought my horse. I ride my horse, feed our cattle when the grazing is not too good, and tend to our pet goat," she answered.

Herman flipped through Carol's medical record to see the blood lab sheets "Tell me about your horse and goat, what are their names?"

"Cinnamon is my horse's name, and I call my goat Billie."

The two of them, doctor, and patient, were having a conversation as pleasant as poetry, like two college freshmen meeting in the pie shop for the first time.

While Herman reviewed Carol Smith's lab work and thought about what tests and procedures he would recommend, he asked, "Carol, tell me about your goat. Is it a male or female?"

"She's a female. Billie had two kids before we got her from friends."

"Do you milk her?"

"Yes, the milk is good. The taste of it varies though, depending upon what Billie eats," she explained. "If she eats clover the milk is sweet, but not so if she consumes grass or weeds."

"Did you go to the farm recently to milk Billie?" Herman asked with a smile.

"Why, uhm, why yes, I did so just uhm, a week ago, before I became ill," Carol replied. Carol's words hung in the air - like a suspended milkweed pod.

Herman patted Carol's arm. As he rose, with his eyes Herman signaled Rachel to bring Carol's parents back into the room, to talk to them.

"I have seen this type of fever before at Walter Reed Medical Center," Herman began. "Sometimes it is caused by an infection from bacteria that might have come from an animal. The incubation period after exposure is from one week to several months, so this fits. The up and down fever spikes are what give brucellosis its colloquial name, undulant fever. Sweats, joint aches, fatigue, muscle aches, loss of appetite, headaches, weight loss - all can occur. The disease causes the body's immune system to fight it by summoning an army of white blood cells resulting in an elevated temperature. It may be the goat." Herman summarized.

Herman then related, "I am recommending to Dr. Cashman that certain tests be ordered. There are some new antibiotics. Streptomycin is one that could be effective to treat brucellosis. So immediately after the tests are done, the drug should probably be started as soon as possible if Dr. Cashman agrees."

Herman said he would be back after dinner. "Mr. Anderson, can you have a vet get a blood sample from Billie, and have the vet's lab do a bacteria culture test as soon as possible?"

"Sure," George said, feeling relieved that some progress was being made, and grateful for the soothing, professional manner of this infectious disease specialist.

Herman stepped into the nurse's station to finish his consultation report. He thanked Rachel and said he would be back at 7 pm. He then called Jake, informing him that he thought Carol contracted brucellosis from a pet goat, and told him what he had recommended.

"It will take it a while for her to get better, but I think we are on the right track," Herman said. Next, Herman called Doctor Cashman and let him know the results of his examination, his working diagnosis, and what tests he had recommended being ordered. Doctor Cashman thanked Doctor Jackson, raised a few questions, and asked him to continue to manage Carol's treatment. Dr. Cashman asked to speak to Rachel. Herman could hear that the tests and medications Herman had wanted were to be implemented.

✧　✧　✧

After dinner, Herman returned to see Carol. Looking over the chart, he was confident that his working diagnosis of brucellosis was the correct one. He was still waiting for the serology test of the blood serum, the clear fluid that separates when the blood clots. The test would tell him if antibodies to the brucellosis bacteria were present in Carol's blood. He also wanted to know the results of testing the pet goat. Herman shared his thoughts with Carol and her parents, who thanked him for his insight and feedback. The next morning Herman returned to see Carol. As he examined her lymph nodes on the side of her neck, checked for pain in her joints, and noted any temperature changes, he asked her about Queen's University. She in turn asked him about running track in high school and playing football at Johnson Smith University.

Carol asked, "Why didn't you play pro football instead of going to Michigan University and later to Meharry Medical School?"

"The simple answer is I wanted to help people like you get better, rather than chase glory on the football field. My grandfather was a slave. He ran away seeking freedom in Canada. After all his struggles, he ended up dying from an infection during the Spanish Flu pandemic. I saw as a young boy how the virus devastated his body as he became overcome with fever. I made a commitment then to treat patients whenever a pathogen like a bacterium or a virus entered the body. I wanted to prevent infections from becoming another pandemic.".

"Could it happen again? I mean another pandemic," Carol asked curiously.

"Yes, it could. There are millions of viruses, bacteria, fungi, and parasites, and they are constantly changing. Carol, have you ever watched a campfire when you ran out of wood? What happened?" Herman asked.

"We have campfires all the time at the farm. We roast marshmallows. When it's late, and we do not put more wood on the fire, it dies," she responded.

"That is the same thing that happens with these bugs. They need fuel to survive and grow. If you stop the transmission from one animal to another, or one human to another, the infectious bugs go away." Herman explained like he was teaching biology class. Patient and doctor, without realizing it, we're experiencing a common interest. They were enjoying the process of relating to each other, despite the prejudices surrounding them. Without being aware, they were reaching a deeper understanding.

✧   ✧   ✧

At Charlotte Memorial Hospital, the Doctor's Lounge was a place where physicians could relax over a cup of coffee and share stories, views about world affairs, and sporting events, and occasionally professional advice. Conversations that could be lively involving up to ten to fifteen physicians, were often punctuated by loud laughter and acted as a tonic for the stress of their jobs. Such was the case the following Monday when conversations went from pro football to what they did over the weekend …, to rumors.

"Hey Cashman, how is your patient doing with that colored doc? I heard they are getting along dandy. I suspect she and he will be here for a while," said Doctor Gordon, a slender general practitioner with thick glasses, brown hair, and a face full of freckles, who was originally from Alabama. Other doctors chimed in to offer disparaging remarks, implying an improper doctor-patient relationship between Herman Jackson MD and his patient. Just then Doctor Spencer entered the room, hearing some of the conversations. He poured himself a cup of coffee, grabbed a section of the newspaper, and said a few quiet hellos. Doctor Spencer sat his rather large frame down on the couch as the cushions deflated.

Doctor Gordon continued, "Why the hell, Cashman, did you not consult a doctor on our staff? Did that Doctor even go to medical school here in the States, or to one in the jungle with a thatched grass roof?"

Smiles and laughter followed. Doctor Cashman sat like a statue. Then after a period of silence, Doctor Spencer rose slowly, like a mountain rising, his face red like an erupting volcano. He tossed his newspaper on the floor and cornered Doctor Gordan, who stood abruptly against the wall. Dr. Spencer shouted, "You pin head, that physician could have made a lot of money playing professional football! Instead, he got his master's degree in epidemiology, graduated first in his class in medical school, then did a residency in internal medicine and a fellowship in infectious disease at Walter Reed General Hospital. He is more than qualified in diagnosing Doctor Cashman's patient, and she is on the mend. The only reason he is not on our staff is not his credentials or abilities! It is the color of his skin!"

The room was as quiet as a church funeral. Doctor Spencer looked around daring anyone to challenge him, and then he left the room. Others followed, like a snake shedding its skin. They wanted to leave their guilt for participating in such a conversation at the door.

As the weeks went by, Carol slowly recuperated under the watchful eye of Doctor Jackson, who came to see her every morning and evening. Unfounded rumors rose that his interest in her was more than professional. Being the only black doctor, eyes were always upon him when he walked through the corridor on the third floor, or in the cafeteria when he got a cup of coffee. Herman avoided these curious eyes like a running back returning a punt. People who saw him witnessed his erect posture, pleasant manner, and his confidence. Herman never let on that he felt the unfair weight of prejudice all around him.

✧   ✧   ✧

A Dark Cloud Approaches

One night as Herman was approaching his car at the far dark side of the parking lot, hatred stuck out its ugly head. Three men attacked, throwing a blanket over Herman. They punched and kicked Herman repeatedly as he lay on the ground.

"Nigger, this is not your place." Herman heard boots hitting his body. With a burst of energy built into his DNA from his grandfather's mistreatment, Herman threw off the blanket and wildly punched at the air, hitting his assailants on the shoulders then on their faces, while being kicked and punched as he did so. Blood, spurting out of his lip and nose, joined the blood of his attackers. An Armageddon occurred between hate and ignorance and the fists of retribution and justice. As quickly as it began, the assault ended. Someone yelling loudly was hurrying toward the scene. The attackers ran away, as Herman collapsed.

A security guard patrolling the parking lot had heard the attack and was the first to reach Herman. He radioed Charlotte Memorial's Emergency Room for assistance, called the police, and attempted to help Herman get to his feet. Soon a team of nurses and interns arrived from the Emergency Room. Carefully they lifted the semiconscious Herman onto a gurney and rushed him back to the Hospital. They ignored a clerk, who asked if Herman should be transferred to Good Samaritan Hospital, which was their standard practice for patients of color. Nurses, interns, and residents knew Herman. He often had entered the hospital through the ER, saying hello as he made his way to the third floor. News of the attack soon spread not only through the Hospital but also to a Charlotte Observer newspaper reporter, Peter Lafferty, who was monitoring his police radio. He soon pieced together that this wasn't just a routine run-of-the-mill assault. It was a hate crime by a bunch of White bigoted men, who attacked Doctor Jackson because they thought he had an improper relationship with a White patient.

Somebody called Margarita. Nurse Rachel got word of it as well on her way out of the hospital. Moments later they were both at Herman's bedside as he regained full consciousness. Then the ER doors from the hallway swung open in a rush of wind and sound. Doctor Spencer surged into the ER with his unbuttoned lab coat floating behind him.

"What happened?" Doctor Spencer commanded, as he pulled back the curtain to Herman's cubicle.

"He was attacked by several men in the parking lot," a nurse said.

Minutes later two police cars arrived, lights flashing. The Emergency Room was in chaos.

✧ ✧ ✧

Peter Lafferty was busy interviewing the security guard and several nurses, who spoke under the condition that their names are not used. The reporter wrote it all down in his notepad. The guard was sure the attackers were White. This was going to be a feature story. A Black doctor was attacked outside of Charlotte Memorial Hospital by three White men. Peter would call it a hate crime. The article would describe in detail the attack of Herman Jackson M.D. Here was a native of Charlotte from the Brooklyn section, a former local football standout, and a teacher. Here was a man who gave service to his country in the Army, who had sterling credentials, including a master's degree, graduating first in his class in medical school, completing a residency and a fellowship with distinction. Yet this physician was denied admission to Charlotte Memorial Hospital's Medical Staff. Peter would elaborate that Doctor Jackson was the Director of Infectious Disease at Good Samaritan Hospital, built and operated for the treatment of colored folks. Peter would write that because of his expertise, the doctor was asked to examine a very ill young White young girl from a wealthy family who was hospitalized at Charlotte Memorial. Now this very accomplished and valuable physician, when leaving the Hospital after seeing his patient, had been brought within inches of dying from injuries caused by prejudice and hate.

The next day as readers absorbed the article, they were overwhelmed by the civil rights slant to it. The segregation of the healthcare system in Charlotte for both patients and physicians alike were now in the open. It seemed unbearable.

Intolerable was most definitely the opinion of Doctor Jake Spencer. He was determined to do something about it. *The hell with tradition.*

George Anderson, who heard of the attack that night as he and his wife Grace were leaving the Hospital, had a similar view. George called Doctor Spencer the next day. "Jake, I would like to discuss at our Hospital's next Board meeting a bylaw amendment that would allow Charlotte Memorial to admit qualified Negro doctors to our medical staff. Can we work together, lobbying those members of the Board who are stuck in the past, and get this segregation issue resolved?"

Jake said, "I agree. By admitting well-trained black doctors and patients of color, we will be benefiting all the people of Charlotte. I can talk to a few Board members who I know."

In three days, Herman recovered from his wounds enough to walk with a limp and resume his treatment of Carol. He still had a shiner over his right eye, his ribs were sore, and he had pain in his hips.

✧　✧　✧

Board Meeting Charlotte Memorial Hospital

On a Wednesday evening at the end of the routine subsequent Board meeting, twelve members sat around a large mahogany table looking proud of themselves for the growth of Charlotte Memorial Hospital. Nothing had been mentioned regarding the parking lot attack. Chairman Arthur Comstock asked if there was any further business. Those members of the Board that had been approached and persuaded by Jake and George knew what was coming. Like a stone thrown in a placid lake, it was then that the predictability and calmness of the proceedings were disrupted.

George Anderson spoke, "I am sure most of you have read about the incident of a Black physician who was attacked in our parking lot after treating one of our patients. You may not be aware, the doctor, a highly trained specialist, was given temporary privileges to treat my daughter, whose life I feared was coming to an end."

Like a pitcher going through his windup before a big pitch, George filled his lungs with air and paused for a long moment... "The police are investigating this matter as a hate crime."

"Speaking as a Board member, I find it abhorrent that we have a policy of denying qualified physicians like Doctor Herman Jackson, who completed a graduate degree in epidemiology, graduated with distinction from medical school, did a residency in internal medicine, and a fellowship in infectious disease, admission to our medical staff, because he is not a member of the Mecklenburg Medical Society. It is well known that our local Medical Society denies membership to physicians of African descent. We need to amend our bylaws to allow both Negro patients to be treated and Negro physicians to practice here. If we allow this segregation practice to stand, we are complicit in harming all the citizens of Charlotte. I will not be a part of this Board if it continues to do so," George concluded. Silence goose-stepped through the room as Board members looked around as if George was talking to someone else.

After a long pause, the elected President of the Medical Staff, Doctor Benjamin commented as if he was reading from the bible, "Well, I am sorry for what happened to Doctor Jackson, and I have heard he has successfully diagnosed your daughter's ailment, George, and is restoring her to health. Our Hospital has built its reputation on certain traditions. Being a part of our Mecklenburg Medical Society is one of the ways we properly screen the character of physicians wishing to join our medical staff. Our physicians are all Society members. We enjoy the professional camaraderie and conferences sponsored by the Medical Society. And we belong to the Society as a group where we share ideas and best practices."

Jake Spencer had asked to be invited to the Board meeting, and now spoke in a voice that bellowed like it was coming out of a cannon, "Dr. Benjamin, to be blunt, that is a bunch of cow manure. The Mecklenburg Medical Society, because they do not need to accept large amounts of money from investors, incur substantial debts, or receive money from the city, state, or federal government for hospital construction funds, does not fear any repercussions from such racist discriminatory practices. But, as you know Doctor Benjamin, we are a not-for-profit hospital, chartered for the benefit of all citizens of Charlotte. Furthermore, there is no recourse that would allow us to take this matter up to the American Medical Society because they have repeatedly voted to leave it up to the local medical societies to decide on their membership requirements. These requirements differ depending upon where you are. I say it is high time to end the Mecklenburg Medical Society's lock on our Hospital. The time has come to enhance our patients' ability to enjoy the benefits of physicians who meet our standards of excellence, not some arbitrary racial requirement."

A lively discussion followed. A lawyer and board member, Ivan Greenfield, said, "The current policy, not only has moral and political problems, but it also leaves the hospital naked to claims that it is acting against federal legislation. The Equal Protection Clause of the 14th Amendment ratified in 1868, and Hill-Burton Act recently passed in 1946 proclaim that any hospital receiving construction funds must make its services available to all persons residing in the area regardless of that person's race, creed, or color. The law permits an exception only in those localities where separate health facilities were planned for different populations if the services were of equal quality."

Doctor Spencer responded in another forceful voice, "One can hardly argue that the Negro only Good Samaritan Hospital is of equal quality to our Hospital. It is time to end this now, **now**! The Charlotte Observer newspaper, in a recent article by Peter Lafferty, exposed our hypocrisy. And last Sunday the ministers of the black Baptist churches called for action. This is not going away."

Chairman Comstock called for order and asked if there was a motion before the board. Attorney Greenfield read a motion, and the board voted to amend the bylaws, granting any qualified physician membership to the medical staff without regard to gender, race, creed, or membership in the Mecklenburg Medical Society. Furthermore, the bylaws were further amended to state that Charlotte Memorial Hospital would treat all patients without discrimination.

Chapter Nineteen

REFLECTION OF A MAVERICK

O N MY WAY out of the hospital after leaving the lab, I made it a custom to stop by and see how the patient in room 310 was doing. Many times, I saw Doctor Jackson at her bedside pouring over lab reports, looking at her chart, and talking to her in a comforting manner. Finally, the fever broke, and the pain subsided in her joints. The brucellosis bacteria were defeated and after several weeks she left our Hospital. When I was with the Marines, I witnessed many losing battles in Nicaragua between the government forces and rebels, so I was glad that this battle ended successfully. I never quite understood the bond between Herman Jackson M.D. and his patient Carol. They both had great empathy for each other. She for the prejudices he and his community in Brooklyn experienced, and he for Carol's pain and suffering she received from a debilitating disease transmitted by the milk from a pet goat. Understanding unconditional nonphysical love is something completely foreign to me. My wife threw me out during my Pathology Residency, proclaiming I cared more for the bugs in the lab and the diseases hidden in dead bodies than for her. She failed to understand how the secrets of the deceased benefited the living, and I took for granted her unconditional love for me.

Carol attended veterinary school at Duke University. Following graduation, she joined a practice in Charlotte. She was active in the women's auxiliary at Good Samaritan Hospital, serving as the auxiliary's president for one year. She was also responsible for two of the Hospital's small additions, resulting from her tireless fundraising activities.

Nevertheless, through the 1950s, as more of its patients went to Charlotte Memorial Hospital for more specialized care, Good Samaritan found it difficult to pay the cost of modern equipment. Through the years additional funds to keep Good Samaritan Hospital solvent came from the Duke Endowment, the Julius Rosenwald Fund, and the Women's Auxiliary. Just as medical economics forced Saint Peter's Hospital to close when Charlotte Memorial Hospital opened in 1940, in 1959 Charlotte Memorial agreed to take over Good Samaritan Hospital. Still later, the ownership of Good Samaritan passed to the City of Charlotte. The integration of hospitals like Charlotte Memorial throughout the South caused the death of hospitals built specially to take care of African Americans. African American folks had access to specialized care in these integrated hospitals, but many could not afford the services. Also, few physicians wanted to take care of them for follow-up care when they became discharged. Eventually, some African American patients lacking primary health care came back to hospitals like Charlotte Memorial through their emergency rooms as their conditions worsened or they contracted other ailments.

African Americans often lived in overcrowded housing, many had poor diets, and some had substandard drinking water, as well as a lack of preventive health care. As a result, African Americans and other minorities often were the first to get infectious diseases. Penicillin, our first real ammunition against bacteria, has been a big help, but many of the respiratory flu viruses spread rapidly and the antibiotics we used were of little help. The creation of the World Health Organization in 1948 has greatly raised the consciousness of the need for better sanitary conditions to control diseases like malaria and yellow fever. However, it is hard to get the healthy, rich countries and wealthy individuals in our country to understand that the most vulnerable among us are the weakest link in maintaining global health. Because of the rapid movement of people, strains of flu from Asia travel to the Americas as fast as a jet plane. We can live in high-rise skyscrapers or gated communities, but like falling dominoes, we are all vulnerable if some of us are vulnerable. If only experts like Herman Jackson M.D. could convince the politicians of the vast return on any investment to improve public health and on research on the prevention of infectious disease. We are not prepared to fight outbreaks of communicable diseases, because people forget the high cost associated with pandemics. I remember reading about the Spanish Flu in medical school. How it infected one-third of the world's population, killing 50 million people, and devastating the global economy. Research regarding how pathogens evolve and how best to prevent localized events from becoming epidemics is essential. Moreover, training leaders like Herman Jackson M.D. in infectious disease is essential to improving our response to pathogens, as well as convincing the public and government to invest in prevention.

The history of the American Medical Association, the body that is supposed to represent the thinking of all physicians, is one of which I am not proud. Herman Jackson, M.D., and numerous other physicians of color have shown us the benefit of having doctors who, because of their backgrounds, are better able to see the causes of illness than some of their other colleagues. Moreover, we have learned that patients are more trusting and more likely to follow the advice of doctors who, because of their similar ethnicity, are better able to empathize with them. I have never understood the AMA's position on leaving the issue of admitting Negro physicians up to the local medical society in the interest of keeping harmony between the northern and southern factions of their society. Sometimes, damn it, you just must do what is right. Take the punches that follow for the health of your organization not just for today, but even more for the organization's long-term reputation and effectiveness in the future.

I am grateful though that the current leadership of the American Medical Association appears to be willing to right some of the wrongs of the past.

Recently, John Nelson, President, of the AMA, gave a speech to the National Medical Association, an organization of Black physicians, in which he apologized for the AMA's discrimination against Negro doctors, not only about membership, but also with regards to their limiting of the number of practicing Black doctors by closing medical schools that graduated mostly Negro physicians.

I am pleased today that the Medical Society of Mecklenburg County is admitting Herman to their society. He was already admitted to the Charlotte Memorial Hospital staff after they stopped requiring membership in the local medical society. I am also grateful that our Hospital has been treating more patients of African descent.

I, Jake Spencer, M.D., former Captain in the US Marines, am proud and fortunate to do the work I love, as Chief of Pathology and the Laboratory at Charlotte Memorial Hospital.

Epilogue

THE MEDICAL SOCIETY and hospitals in North Carolina are fully integrated now as part of the 1964 Civil Rights Act, which ended segregation in public places and banned employment discrimination based on race, color, religion, sex, or national origin. African Americans, however, are more likely to be employed in occupations where employer-sponsored health insurance is less common. Not being able to afford good primary care through insurance or from their disposable income makes it difficult for African Americans to obtain care. Often the only source of primary care for persons of color, other than through Medicaid, is an inadequately funded Neighborhood Health Clinic or being seen in the Emergency Room, where the cost of primary care is much more than a trip to a private doctor. The same prejudices that resulted in the segregation of hospitals during the Jim Crow era, led to congressmen from the southern states voting against universal healthcare in 1947. More recently many legislatures from those same states voted not to expand the Medicaid program as part of the Affordable Care Act. Some feel they did not want to spend the money to provide healthcare for more of its citizens, even though doing so would raise the health of the most vulnerable and lessen the spread of any communicable disease.

Speaking in Chicago before the Committee for Human Rights, Martin Luther King in 1966 perhaps said it best when he proclaimed, "Of all the forms of inequality, injustice in healthcare is the most shocking and inhumane."

As we have learned, societies that do not protect their most vulnerable become vulnerable themselves to catastrophic pathogens that lead to pandemics. Humans are evolving in a constant battle against viruses, bacteria, fungi, and parasites, which are all mutating, all struggling for survival. Some pathogens lose their virulence over time, others become more aggressive and find ways to jump from animal hosts to human ones. A bug in 1890 mutated and passed from a Russian cow to humans and spread to become a pandemic killing over 1 million people. This organism's deadly infectious effects on mankind then weakened over time to become no more than a common cold today. There is nothing to stop this same virus from changing, once again becoming more lethal, making it even harder to stop in today's world. Infectious disease is all about the march of evolution and how we prepare all our citizens for the battles that are sure to come. Given the cost of the current COVID-19 pandemic to the world's economy and the deaths it has caused, a small investment to prevent such a calamity would seem warranted.

Acknowledgments

MY LOVE OF history was ignited while traveling through Europe after college. While there I visited Dachau, the German concentration camp. I was amazed how the camp was left mostly as it was at the end of World War II. In the museum built as part of the camp, I saw numerous pictures on the walls, and I watched a movie depicting the Holocaust and the role that concentration camps played in it. I questioned why the German people would want to showcase this horrific place of their past. Then before my exit, I noticed a small plaque on a blank wall. It invited me over to read it before leaving. On it were the words by a Spanish philosopher George Santayana, *"Those who cannot remember the past are condemned to repeat it."* I knew then why the German people had allowed Dachau to stand, not so much for the world to see, but for present and future generations of Germans. So, they might see and learn from their past. I hope this book is perhaps telling you something as well.

It is a work of fiction based loosely on the life of Doctor Emory Louvelle Rann Jr., who was born on March 9, 1914, and died on September 14, 1996. He was the first Black physician accepted into the Mecklenburg County Medical Society, and one of the first Negro Doctors to receive hospital privileges at Charlotte Memorial Hospital. It did not come easily. Dr. Rann Jr did receive membership in the Medical Society, like the character of Herman Jackson MD.. In real life, there were student marches that raised awareness, but did not produce integration. To get the North Carolina Medical Society to admit black physicians, Doctor Rann Jr., joined by a black dentist and minister, Doctor Reginald Hawkins, appealed to U.S. Attorney Robert Kennedy to intervene. They asked Kennedy to lend his support because hospitals in North Carolina had received Hill-Burton funds. These funds required hospitals to provide equal treatment and not discriminate. Immediately on hearing that Kennedy was sending a fact-finding mission, John Rankin, Charlotte Memorial Hospital Administrator, announced its doors would be open to all. Dr. Rann Jr's work on medical desegregation put him also in contact with Doctor Montague Cobb, a surgeon, and professor at Howard University. Doctors Rann Jr. and Cobb, along with others, formed the Imhotep Conference to eliminate segregation in the healthcare field.

I chose the title Salt Wagon because it was representative of how an African American family helped to free Samuel Meharry's wagon from a ditch during a storm. This simple act of unexpected kindness years later led to Samuel's generous donation and the founding of Meharry Medical School, an institution dedicated to training African Americans and others in the medical field. The subtitle of *The struggle for acceptance* was added to dramatize the conflict, not only of Herman Jackson M.D. to be accepted into the Mecklenburg Medical Society and Charlotte Memorial Hospital, but also to highlight the challenges descendants of slaves have faced. To showcase the latter, throughout Salt Wagon, I tried using my characters to sprinkle true events and history. For instance, the journey of runaway slaves John and Loretta through what was called the Underground Railroad, exemplified the perseverance of runaway slaves and generosity of folks to assist them with their journey to freedom. Also, by relating some details of a tank battalion of Negro soldiers called the Black Panthers I tried to show the contributions of African Americans during War World II. I wanted the mistakes made during the Spanish Flu pandemic to be a window through which we could see how to handle future outbreaks of infectious disease. Lastly, I wanted to show from history how segments of the population, like some African Americans, by not having access to adequate primary healthcare, can become vulnerable to infectious diseases and other ailments. This in turn can increase the potential that the entire population may become vulnerable. Revealing some of the mistakes made during the pandemic of 1918 was done not to slight our public health response, but to showcase, like Dachau, that the United States can learn from past mistakes. Judging from our recent mortality experience with Covid 19 in comparison with other countries, it would appear we could do better. Perhaps we could learn from other countries that have had fewer deaths from the virus per population. (According to the United States, COVID Coronavirus Statistics-Worldometer as of December 18, 2021, 827,206 deaths have occurred in the US. To compare this with other countries one must look at COVID deaths per one million population. For the US it is 2,478 as of this date, compared with 786 for Canada, 146 for Japan, 92 for South Korea, and 10 for New Zealand. In other words, at that point in time, one is 3 times more likely to die in the US than in Canada from COVID-19, 17 times more likely to die in the US from the virus than in Japan, and 247 times more likely to die from COVID in the US than in New Zealand.)

I am indebted to a former Presbyterian minister who grew up in Charlotte, Bruce Chapman, who inspired me to write this novel by sharing information about Dr. Rann, Jr., and Good Samaritan Hospital. His spirituality and moral compass have always been a good example to me, his family, my son Jason, his wife Jordan, and students. Others who helped me shape the story included William Olney, M.D. Appreciation is greatly extended to Corinne Prete and Michael Wrigley, M.D. for their support and editing. Also, my thanks go to Elizabeth Soares for her help in formatting the document and to William Sudah, as well as the design team at Experts Subjects for their assistance with the cover and getting the book into print. I especially wish to recognize the contributions of Bill Benoit, whose artistic talents made the cover of the book so special.

The events that took place at Charlotte Memorial Hospital were fictional, although Doctor Rann Jr. was denied admission to the medical staff of the Hospital on the basis that he was not a member of the Mecklenburg Medical Society. Through the Nurse Manager, Rachel, I tried to show the dedication of nurses to their patients. I am sure the present-day nurses and physicians as part of the larger Atrium Health have the same commitment to quality of care. (I should know since my daughter-in-law during her delivery of our two adorable grandkids received such excellent compassionate care there.)

As the pandemic of 2019 to 2022 has taught us, the benefits of integrating the medical field and bringing equal access to primary health care to all people cannot be overstated. On one hand, physicians benefit by sharing best practices, and having different sensitivities when looking at the same problem. On the other hand, more patients benefit from having access to affordable care, because they are able to avoid serious illnesses. These same patients may also become less vulnerable to communicable diseases, or not be forced into bankruptcy to treat a loved one.

I am also grateful to professors in the Yale University School of Medicine, Department of Epidemiology and Public Health. These teachers, during my graduate studies, increased my awareness of how the disparities in income and access to primary health care cause the most vulnerable in our society to suffer more when pandemics strike. Recently the President of the Association of Yale Alumni in Public Health, Kathe Fox, Ph.D., described how the pandemic affected residents in her home city:

> *"I live in Baltimore, MD, a city that is primarily non-white and economically poor, surrounded by wealthy suburbs. During the early days of vaccinations, more than 50% of individuals being vaccinated in Baltimore City did not live here because of the high concentrations of healthcare workers at Johns Hopkins and the University of Maryland. Working-class residents who had continued to work in risky, low-paying*

jobs often could not access vaccinations; these were the non-institutionalized people who were getting sick and dying. These were the families who were trying to juggle working while their children were going to school "virtually" in homes without computers or internet access. This pandemic revealed the harsh inequities of haves and have-nots. It made cities like Baltimore examine, as never before, the deficiencies in their social welfare infrastructure. At every turn the State of Maryland would issue a Covid mandate which had to be modified because Baltimore City was not at the same level as the rest of the State; infections, positivity rates, deaths, vaccination access, all moved more slowly or quickly than the rest of the State and presented unique challenges."

The benefits of research and early intervention to decrease epidemics were also stressed during my graduate work in epidemiology and public health. Now research into viruses is somewhat fragmented, and not all labs have the same security and safety measures. Imagine, if research, embracing the highest of safety practices, could be coordinated globally. Imagine research motivated not by government awards, or the profits of pharmaceutical firms. Rather research could be coordinated to identify pathogens from animals, leading to the development of vaccines to be inventoried and ready. Once an outbreak occurs, these vaccines could be auctioned off to pharmaceutical companies for production and distribution in an equitable manner, so that all people would have access to their benefits, not just wealthy residents.

Since we are all in this together, funding for infectious disease prevention and treatment, and especially pandemic drug research and development, ideally should be shared by all countries on an ongoing basis, so vaccines and other beneficial drugs can be produced and deployed quickly, not long after a pandemic starts.

There are many options for sources of such funding over and above what may be received from large pharmaceutical companies that bid on a vaccine already discovered by smaller and, in some cases, non-commercial vaccine development entities. Two factors to be considered about equitable country funding contributions to drug development costs and drug distribution sharing would be 1) the proportion of a country's population to the world's population and 2) the country's GNP relative to the world's total GNP.

A carbon fee or tax may additionally be a partial answer to funding pandemic-related research, preparation, and treatment. Many believe a major contributor to pandemics is the heating of our planet. As temperatures rise polar ice melts, coastal areas flood, and more droughts, forest fires, and other extreme natural disasters occur. As a result of these environmental changes, significant amounts of housing space and agricultural land becomes unsuitable, which forces people to live closer together, and, at the same time, nearer to wild animals. This increases the probability of transmission of disease. Deforestation is also occurring which causes animals to migrate in search of suitable habitats or cooler temperatures, potentially sharing pathogens with other animals or people. Moreover, many pathogens thrive in tropical climates. Excess heat breeds ticks and mosquitos which lead to many communicable diseases.

Joint therapeutic drug development for infectious diseases is another area that could benefit from a more collaborative effort. During Operation Warp Speed our government put a priority on the development of a vaccine for the prevention of COVID-19. This was successful. Unfortunately, communicable diseases like COVID-19 require extensive clinical trials, not only to show the safety of the drug or its deleterious side effects but also to show that it produces the desired outcome. Many of the studies of these potential drugs were funded by our government, generating vast amounts of data. It was reported in the New England Journal of Medicine in April 2021, however, by Dr. Harlan Kimholtz and others, that about 2 billion dollars were spent by the National Institutes of Health for research on COVID drugs. Ninety-two percent of those clinical trials were not completed or had not yet released their data. The clinical trial information was proprietary, and not widely shared in an open-source and collaborative fashion. Thus, the data collected did not contribute to the successful search for new effective drugs as much as it could have if a more coordinated and open approach had been followed.

It is not enough to just coordinate the development of vaccines, we need to increase our capacity to produce them in large quantities once vaccines are formulated, created, made in quantities enough to be carefully and thoroughly tested, and proven safe and effective. Wealthy countries, where most of the world's pharmaceutical and biomedical companies reside, produce disproportionately more vaccines, and often earmark the distribution of them to their own residents. They also can, and some first-world countries do, have an efficient plan to have enough of their population vaccinated to achieve herd immunity. Poor countries, by contrast, have little or no pipeline to produce the needed supply. In fact, according to the May issue of *The Economist,* the Covid Vaccine Global Access Facility, COVAZ, a vaccine sharing mechanism for pooled procurement and equitable distribution of COVID-19 vaccines, only 59 million doses of Covid vaccines were provided to low-income countries by the spring of 2021. If the most vulnerable in these poor countries do not get vaccinated, the risk increases that the virus will mutate and develop variants (like the Delta and Omicron variants) that spread to residents of wealthier countries.

A global commitment is needed to expand production rapidly once a pandemic is foreseen. In March the journal *Scientist* said that if the world had collaborated to provide a global infrastructure of vaccination capable of bringing the planet up to herd immunity, the world's economy would have been greater by 5 trillion dollars.

Spending smartly on infectious disease treatment and prevention research may save us some time in the future from the recurrence of some of the immense costs we recently experienced during the COVID-19 pandemic. The cost of increasing production later in a pandemic's cycle costs far more, and the delay has a greater damaging effect on the health of the population and economies of the world.

Scientists warn that pandemics are likely to occur more often, causing, if not prevented through extensive human efforts or caught in time, trillions of dollars of economic losses and millions of unnecessary deaths.

Sources

In writing this work of fiction I used several sources described below as reference material.

Journal of the American Medical Association, 1964, May 56 (3) pg. 226 -229

Charlotte Mecklenburg Historic Land Commission; *Old Good Samaritan Hospital,* March 6, 1985.

Rev. Newberry, *Obituary for Emery Loubelle Rann Jr.,* Memorial Presbyterian Church, Charlotte, NC Accessed January 15, 2021, through http://wwwmccrosrey.historysouth.org

Charles H. Ambler, *A History of West Virginia* pg. 276-79

Lindsay Van Dyk, *Shaping a Community: Black Refugees in Nova Scotia,* Accessed February 15, 2021, through https://pier21.ca/research/immigrationhistory/shapingacommunity-blackrefugiesinnovascotia

Carter G. Woodson, *Early Negro Education in West Virginia* Accessed February 16, 2021, through www.WVculture.org/history/africanamericans/woodsoncarter02.html

A Brief Synopsis of Medical School, (2017) Accessed by March 20, 2021, through
http://www.peterson.com/blog/a-brief-synopsisofmedical-school

Murray Atkins Library, *Historic Brooklyn Community,* Accessed April 26, 2021, through
https//guides.library.uncc.edu/c.php?g=621704&p=4626874

Vernon, John (2008) *Jim Crow meet Lieutenant Robinson,* Prologue Magazine, National Archives and Records (NARA) 40 (1)

761 Tank Battalion, Accessed by May 20, 2021, through
https//en.wikipedia.org/
wiki/761ist_tank_Battalion_(UnitedStates)#cite_ref-business

Nashville's Civil Rights Movement, Accessed by May 21, 2021, through historicnashvilleinc.org

Panhuis, William MD, Grefenstette Ph.D., Jug S, *Contagious Disease in the United States from 1888 to present,* Accessed May 20, 2021, through *ccbi.nim.nih.gov*

The Salt Wagon Story, Accessed by May 25, 2021, through https://www.mmc.edu/about/saltwagon-story.htm

Hauck, Grace, *We're Celebrating Thanksgiving Amid a Pandemic. Here is how we did it in 1918 and what Happened Next.* USA Today, Nov. 21, 2020, Updated Nov. 24, 2020

November 20, 1935: The New York Committee of Vigilance Founded, Accessed by April 16, 2021, through zinnedproject.org

Why the 1918 Flu Pandemic Never Ended History, Accessed by April 17, 2021, through
https://www.history.com/news/1918-flu-pandemic-neverended

Dodds, Walter, *Diseases Now and the Potential Future Pandemics-The World's Worst Problems,* 2019 Dec 3:31-44, Published Dec 3, 2019, 10.1007/978-3-030-304,10-24 Accessed by May 25, 2021, though http://www.wcbi.nim.wih.gov/pmc/articles/pmc71202001

Ssabetmd Ph.D., Pardis *Natural Selection: Uncovering Mechanisms of Evolution Adaptation to Infection Disease,* Scitable, Accessed by May 28, 2021, through https://www.nature.com/scitable/topicpage/ natural-selection-uncovering-mechanisms

Bruce, David, from Wikipedia, accessed by May 25, 2021, through https://en.wikipedia.org/wiki/david _bruce_(microbiologist)

Sidney, Jonathan, *Exploring the AMA's History of Discrimination,* ProPublica, July 16, 2008, Accessed by May 28, 2021, through https:www.propublica.org/article/ exploring-the-amas-history-of-discrimination-716

The History of African Americans and Organized Medicine, Accessed by May 28, 2021, through https://www.ama-assn.org/about/ama-history/ history-africanamerican-and-organized

Nicaraguan Civil War (1926-27) Wikipedia Accessed by May 30, 2021, through https://en.wikipedia.org/wiki/nicaraguan_civil_war(1926-1927)

Woodson, Carter, *Early Negro Education in West Virginia,* (The West Virginia College Institute, 1921) Accessed by May 30, 2021, through *www.wvculture.org/history/africanamer-icans/woodsoncarter/02.html*

History.com editors, May 4, 2010, *Battle of the Alamo,* updated Jan 12, 2021, Accessed by May 30, 2021 through https:www.history.com/topics/mexicoalamo

Gamble MD Ph.D., Vanessa, *There wasn't a lot of comfort in those days: African American, Public Health, and the 1918 influenza Epidemic,* Public Health Rep 2010: 125(Supp 13):114-122 Accessed by May 30, 2021, through https://www.ncbi.nim.nih.gov/pmc/articles/PMC2862340

Oration: Delivered in Corinthian Hall, Rochester, By Frederick Douglass July 5th, 1852, Accessed by May 30, 2021, through https://rbscp.l.b.rochester.edu/2945

Oakland, Helene and Manelund, Sven Erik, *Race and 1918 Influenza Pandemic in the US: a review of the Literature,* Inc J Environ Res Public Health 2019 Jul: 16 (14) 2487 Accessed by June 1, 2021, through NCBI.NLM.NIH

Prior, Ryan *Here's How to Design Drug Trials to Defeat the Next Pandemic* Accessed by July 5, 2021, through *https://www.cnn.com/2021/07/04/health/drug/-trials-covid-pandemic/index.html.go*

Krishan, Aggarwal, MD, MBA, *The Legacy of James McCune Smith MD-The First US Black Physician, JAMA, December 14, 2021, Volume 326, Number 22 pg. 2245 and 2246.*

United States COVID Coronavirus Statistics_Worldometer as of December 18, 2021, httpsl//www.worldometer.info>coronavirus>country>US

May you always give and receive the unexpected gift of kindness and generosity - the salt wagon that lives in all of us.

About the Author

THOMAS BENOIT is an author who enjoys writing fiction with a historical background. Tom is a former hospital administrator. He founded and presently manages an executive search company, Allen Thomas Associates, Inc., which provides recruiting and consulting services for the healthcare industry.

Tom received his bachelor's degree in business administration from Villanova University and a master's degree in epidemiology and public health from Yale University. From working in hospitals and graduate studies in epidemiology, Tom developed a keen interest in infectious disease and the promotion of optimal health in populations through improved access to primary health.

Tom's first book was a memoir, *Reflections: The Untold Story of an Uncommon Man,* based on his father, Armand, and his ancestors, who came first from France, and then from Arcadia (now Nova Scotia, Canada) before settling in Salem Massachusetts. Tom's second novel, *Just Desserts,* was about his mother, Mary, who just passed away on October 19, 2021, after a long life of one hundred and one years. The struggles of her ancestors, leaving Ireland during the potato famine and finally coming to Lynn Massachusetts, together with Mary's steely strength in raising seven children, as her mother and grand-mother had done, is an inspiration.

Tom considers himself blessed to have a supportive family, which includes his wife, Mary Jane, two sons, Brian with his wife Tory, and Jason with his wife Mary Jordan, as well as four grandchildren: Penelope (Poppy), Elizabeth Jane (Libby), Bill, and Tommy.

The net profits from the sale of this book and any royalties from any movie or audiobook rights will be donated to the education of African American physicians, nurses, physician assistants, and epidemiologists to improve the health of people in their community. Any additional funds will be donated for research into the prevention of infectious diseases.

Made in the USA
Columbia, SC
06 September 2022

65904860R00115